Partnerships for Lifelong Learning

2nd Edition

Lesley S. J. Farmer

A Publication of THE BOOK REPORT & LIBRARY TALK
Professional Growth Series

Linworth Publishing, Inc.
Worthington, Ohio

DEDICATION

To all of my educational partners:
Thanks for helping our youth.

Library of Congress Cataloging-in-Publication Data

Farmer, Lesley S. J.
    Partnerships for lifelong learning / by Lesley S. J. Farmer
         p.   cm.–(Professional growth series)
    "A publication of The Book report & Library talk."
    Rev. ed. of: Creative partnerships. c1993.
    Includes bibliographical references (p.).
    ISBN 0-938865-79-X
    1. School libraries–United States. I. Farmer, Lesley S. J.
    Creative partnerships. II. Book report (Columbus, Ohio)
    III. Library talk. IV. Title.   V. Series.
    Z675.S3F236   1999
    027.8'223'0973–dc21   99-32263
                                                               CIP

Published by Linworth Publishing, Inc.
480 East Wilson Bridge Road, Suite L
Worthington, Ohio 43085

Copyright©1999 by Linworth Publishing, Inc.

Series Information:
    From The Professional Growth Series

All rights reserved. Reproduction of this book in whole or in part, without permission of the publisher, is prohibited except for not-for-profit educational use in the classroom, in the school library, in professional workshops sponsored by elementary and secondary schools, or other similar not-for-profit activities.

ISBN 0-938865-79-X

5 4 3 2 1

Table of Contents

TABLE OF PARTNERSHIP TOOLS... iii
ABOUT THE AUTHOR... iv
CHAPTER 1: Introduction... 1
CHAPTER 2: Setting the Stage... 3
    Where Are We?... 3
    Where Do We Want To Go?... 5
    What are the Gaps?... 5
    Why Partner?... 6
    Why Not Partner?... 9
CHAPTER 3: What Is a Partnership?... 11
    Starting with Yourself... 11
    The Other Person... 13
    Social Interaction... 13
    The Task at Hand... 15
    Meeting Standards via Information Literacy in
        the Library Case Study... 17
    Individuals vs. Groups... 20
    Virtual Partners... 23
CHAPTER 4: Who Is a Partner?... 25
    Classroom Teachers... 25
    Support Staff... 28
    Administrators... 30
    Students... 34
    Parents and Guardians... 36
    Community... 45
    Professional Peers... 50
CHAPTER 5: How Do Partners Grow?... 55
    Groundwork... 55
    The Garden Shows... 56
    Meeting with Groups... 60
    Planting Seeds... 60
    Plotting Partnerships... 63
    Making the Garden Grow... 64
    School Community-Developed Program... 64
    Community-Based Partnership Program... 66
    Pot to Pasture... 71
    Obstacles and Inducements... 72
    Systemic Issues... 73
    When Conflicts Arise... 73
    Personal Issues... 74

Table of Contents continued

	The Impact of Technology............................... 74
	How Does the Partnership Garden Grow? 75
	Life Cycles of Partnerships 79
CHAPTER 6:	Where Do Partners Practice?........................... 81
	Information Literacy Standards......................... 81
	Primary Grades....................................... 83
	Upper Elementary..................................... 83
	Middle School 84
	High School 84
	Teaching and Learning................................. 86
	Integrate the Library Media Program 86
	Integrate Information Literacy Standards 86
	Promote Collaborative Planning and Curriculum Development....... 89
	Access a Full Range of Information Resources and Services........ 91
	Encourage Media Understanding and Enjoyment............... 91
	Support Diverse Learning 94
	Foster Inquiry 95
	Integrate Technology 95
	Link with the Larger Community....................... 96
	Information Access and Delivery....................... 97
	Provide Intellectual Access to Information and Ideas 97
	Provide Physical Access to Resources.................. 98
	Provide a Climate for Learning 98
	Provide Equitable Access 100
	Develop and Evaluate Collections Collaboratively 102
	Promote Intellectual Freedom........................ 103
	Reflect Legal and Professional Practice 104
	Program Administration.............................. 104
	Support the School 105
	Plan Strategically 105
	Do Ongoing Assessment.............................. 106
	Do Ongoing Staff Development 106
	Communicate Clearly 114
CHAPTER 7:	The Partnership Community and Lifelong Learning............ 115
	Changing Roles 115
	Changing Information 116
	Changing Reality 116
BIBLIOGRAPHY	 119
INDEX	 123

Table of Partnership Tools

CHAPTER 2: Setting the Stage
The Planning Process Checklist 7

CHAPTER 3: What Is a Partnership?
A Planning Matrix 14
District Library Plan 21
Internet Team Project: Growing Up in Time 23

CHAPTER 4: Who Is a Partner?
Teacher Planning Tips for Student Success in the Library 27
Sample Equipment Program Report Form 29
TAs in Technology: Course of Study 31
Tutoring Techniques 34
Friends of the Library Flyer 37
Adopt-A-Book Flyer 38
Parent Library Volunteer Letter 39
Job Description for Volunteer Library Aide 40
Apple Partners in Education Grant Proposal 46
Checklist for Partnerships with Local Libraries 50
Library Services and Technology Act Grant Proposal 51

CHAPTER 5: How Do Partners Grow?
Make the Library Connection Survey 58
Library Scavenger Hunt 59
Sample Pathway Guide 62
Sample Workshop: Encouraging Your Child to Read 67
Partnership Rubric 77

CHAPTER 6: Where Do Partners Practice?
Supreme Court Simulation Lesson Plan 85
Research Skills Instruction Chart 88
Collaborative Plan: Hispanic Painters 90
Imaging Music Lesson Plan 92
Online Homework Help Checklist 99
A Model Time Frame for Class Library Research Projects 101
High School Use Survey for Students 107
Workshop Framework 109

About the Author

DR. LESLEY FARMER received her MSLS from the University of North Carolina at Chapel Hill and her doctorate from Temple University in Philadelphia. She has directed public and private school libraries on both coasts. She has taught in library schools in Tunisia, Virginia, Pennsylvania, and California. Dr. Farmer has written hundreds of articles and over a dozen books on library science and presented at state, national and international library conferences. In addition, Dr. Farmer has garnered several professional awards. Presently, she coordinates the school library media services credential program at California State University, Long Beach.

Introduction

*Things turn out better when we work together.
It is a fact that, in the right formation, the lifting power of many
wings can achieve twice the distance of any bird flying alone.*

Information overload. Constant change. Sex, drugs and rock 'n' roll. Dysfunctional families. Kids falling through the cracks. Do I hear someone crying, "Help?"

As we enter the new millennium, one thing is clear: It takes a community of partners to ensure successful preparation for lifelong learning. While school librarians and classroom teachers historically have aimed at the same goal of educating young people, their present-day strategies not only reinforce but also complement and increasingly overlap each other. Librarian teachers have assumed the role of instructional specialists, progressing from "point and read" library skills to rigorous information literacy processes. Classroom teachers must increasingly diagnose and address individual needs, much as librarians have done over the years. Factoring in educational technology and technology specialists, educators find themselves with more work to do and a more diverse population to work with. No one person can do it alone. The entire school community needs to work collaboratively in order to meet the educational challenges of the 21st century.

The 1998 edition of *Information Power: Building Partnerships for Learning* (American Association of School Librarians and the Association for Educational Communications and Technology) underscores the above reality. The authors believe that students need to be actively engaged in authentic learning that forms the foundation for lifelong learning. Each person in the school community, and beyond, contributes to this vision. Specifically, the school library media specialist (the term "school librarian" is the main job title used in the book) brings to the community a cross-curricular perspective about information resources, needs, and delivery systems. He must also recognize the significant roles of other school community members and work proactively with them beyond the traditional realm of the school library.

Such interaction among school members can be intimidating, even daunting. It requires greater knowledge about each other's needs and competencies. It requires rethinking power and influence. It requires constant reforming and negotiating. And it requires more time, especially at the start. A bad experience can cause partners to throw up their hands in frustration, narrow their focus to a couple of partners or activities, and wonder if all this coordination is necessary.

The answer is "yes," and this book examines the issue of partnerships in order to help the school community develop meaningful partnerships that foster effective education. From a librarian-teacher viewpoint, the author offers ways to grow, nurture, and sometimes prune educational relationships.

The following chapter sets the stage for partnership by exploring current educational challenges and their impact on the changing roles of school community members. It deals with contemporary educational goals and gaps and then discusses the benefits and costs of educational partnerships.

The beginning step in successful partnerships is to define what a partner is and does. The third chapter examines social interaction and educational work in light of individuals and groups.

The entire school community consists of potential partners for learning. The fourth chapter demonstrates how each constituency has its own set of characteristics, abilities, needs, and expectations. Implications for librarian teacher partnerships are outlined.

The fifth chapter details the life cycles of partnerships, from formation to finding the right fit. Obstacles and inducements are noted, including the context of technology.

The real test of partnerships is their impact on the learning community. The sixth chapter offers several scenarios in line with *Information Power*.

The seventh chapter deals with short- and long-term impacts of effective partnerships in terms of roles, the nature of information, and educational realities.

A bibliography concludes the book.

School librarians and other teachers want their students to blossom. Working in partnership with the entire school community can lead to a thriving garden of education. Dig in!

> The beginning step in successful partnerships is to define what a partner is and does.

CHAPTER 2

Setting the Stage

*Goals are the bridges that span our dreams.
Co-workers help you get where you want to go.*

- Checking out a camcorder for a French class skit and teaching the aide to use the equipment
- Troubleshooting an Internet connection in the computer lab next door
- Helping a student find a fiction book for a social issues assignment
- Getting out a notice about a school facilities meeting
- Scheduling a special education assessment session
- Writing a grant to get local environmental resources
- Teaching a parent how to file books
- Helping five classes conduct research

That's what a school librarian does in a typical day. Notice all of the possible partners: aide, technology specialist, student, administration, resource specialist, community agency, parent, classroom teacher. To what degree does the school librarian credential encompass all of this activity? To what extent did partnerships figure in this picture? How many of these skills were learned after graduation? For today's school librarian, the learning curve never levels off. He has more than ever to do, but no more time to do it in.

School librarians have worked with classroom teachers for decades, but the social context and the educational picture that reflects it have changed significantly, demanding authentic partnerships with a wide variety of school community members to accomplish meaningful teaching. When schools seem understaffed, partnerships offer a positive way to make effective use of available expertise. In any case, the school has to identify its population, decide on its goals, and determine how to help students.

▷ WHERE ARE WE?

Recently, a parent complained to a district superintendent, "Why can't you just teach the basics? That was fine for me!" The administrator retorted, "A lot has happened in the 20 years or more since you were in high school." There's much more to teach these days: computer science, international conflicts, AIDS, and the list goes on.

In addition, schools have been asked to address more issues than ever before — and are expected to perform. Sex education, parenting, health issues, diversity training, and even simple manners have been added to the school curriculum. Seldom, though, has more time been allocated to cover these areas substantively.

Part of the reason that schools have been called to assume a greater societal role is that society has to contend with more issues with more poorly defined social structures. Consider the percentage of intact traditional families: less than seven percent. With increased social mobility, fewer families have strong community ties. They can't expect that the neighborhood will participate in their young people's lives, especially in an age of AIDS and an atmosphere that favors immediate gratification over long-term investment of time and effort. Technology, too, has impacted society significantly in terms of instant communication, democratization—or deprivation—of information, and automation of manual jobs, and all at a cost of widening the gap between rich and poor.

And then, there are the students themselves and their responses to these realities. In California, for instance, the population is changing to the degree that by 2006 no majority ethnic group will exist. It is estimated that by 2040, Latinos will take over as the most populous ethnic group. Alongside ethnic diversity is the ever-increasing gap between rich and poor. Technology access must now be added to the socioeconomic equation, which not only disadvantages present populations but also limits the educational aspirations for young people. Still another factor is substance abuse: crack babies who are now in the school system, youngsters under the influence of drugs, victims of drug-related crime, and so forth. In addition, social messages about ideal body images have heightened the risk for young people who cope dysfunctionally through eating disorders, steroid abuse, self-mutilation, and even suicide. Regardless of student abilities and needs, the school community has a responsibility to educate all of these diverse populations.

What have schools done in response? They've seen the need for contextual learning along with the need for actively engaged students. Cross-curricular projects are one answer to involvement, but that requires more coordination. A greater variety of informational resources in different formats, delivered in multiple ways, accommodates individual learning styles and needs. More personalization is called for to connect meaningfully with all students and to diagnose and address unique needs. Educators have had to pay more attention to the complex realities of students' lives outside of the classroom, which challenge teachers to maintain high expectations while accommodating various aptitudes and abilities. It's a difficult and frustrating job. In the midst of these social realities, even the most dedicated librarian may feel overwhelmed and say, "I don't want to save the world, just help one child."

Yet, to be effective, school librarians need to participate as partners in assessing a school's present situation in order to proceed. Who is the student population? What are the

> **More personalization is called for to connect meaningfully with all students and to diagnose and address unique needs.**

community conditions and trends? What societal influences shape the school? What is the school's organizational and power structure? What human and material resources are available and how are they utilized? Perspectives from students, staff, parents, and the community at large need to be incorporated. As data gatherers, librarians can ferret out sources. As organizers, they can sort and synthesize data. As researchers, they can provide possible solutions to problems like low reading scores. Librarians can thus work in concert with other educators to develop a clear picture of the school community and make informed decisions about what actions to take. What's at stake? Our children's future.

► WHERE DO WE WANT TO GO?

What are schools "about"? They remain the principal means of preparing young people for the world in which they will live. Educators can identify certain skills, knowledge, and attitudes that students will need in order to succeed in that new age. In fact, a clear picture of desirable student outcomes is necessary for a cohesive, school-wide effort. Typically, a school agrees upon a mission. Then it develops a set of clear, meaningful standards in order to measure whether or not it fulfills that mission.

A variety of tools measure student success—traditionally grades, tests, observations, post-graduation plans, projects, and presentations. To help describe student performance, rubrics may be developed. It is often effective to have several people use different measurements to get at a more comprehensive picture of the student.

As archivists, librarians should have copies of standards and curricula for the entire school community to access and should partner with others to assess student achievement. Consider the number of times that librarians are asked to instruct or coach students during research projects, only to be left out of the assessment loop. If librarians do not see the final results of student work, how can they determine how effective their library program is?

► WHAT ARE THE GAPS?

One of the main reasons for describing the school's mission is to have a basis for identifying educational gaps. Only when the librarian and classroom teacher can decide what students should learn and then assess how well they learned it can educational problems be diagnosed and treated. For instance, library instruction is often oral. If it can be determined that visual learners aren't understanding a concept, then the librarian can incorporate overhead transparencies or guide sheets.

> Only when the librarian and classroom teacher can decide what students should learn and then assess how well they learned it can educational problems be diagnosed and treated.

Of course, determining which strategies to use requires thought and often research. Again, librarians can provide the theoretical underpinnings as well as case studies. Let's take student research projects. Problems can arise at several points. Here are some possible scenarios.

The assignment isn't clear. The librarian may overhear students saying, "I don't understand what I'm supposed to do." Perhaps the teacher is seen explaining the project repeatedly to individual students. Assignments could be analyzed in terms of clarity and specificity. The librarian could work with the teacher by asking clarifying questions to refine the assignment language and directions.

Students can't find the information they need. If the task requires students to find information not available in the library; the librarian could get materials through interlibrary loan, buy needed resources for the next time the assignment is given, or modify the assignment to use available materials. In the future, the librarian and teacher could craft the assignment ahead of time to match expectations with on-site resources.

Students can't access the information they need. This usually indicates they don't know how to use access tools such as indexes, catalogs, or search engines. When students need individual help to use these tools, the librarian can be confident in telling the teacher that direct instruction is needed. In some cases, guide sheets or user signage could complement or supplement such instruction.

Students can't evaluate the sources. They may be unable to determine the author's viewpoint or purpose, choose off-target articles or Internet sites or the wrong materials to answer the research question (for instance, picking a 1963 book on AIDS to find current research or using a magazine index to find a cross-section of an earthworm). Again, direct instruction could be needed. Students could develop criteria and see models for evaluation. Some evaluation techniques are general, such as distinguishing between fact and opinion, but each discipline has its own unique properties which students could learn.

Students don't complete the assignment on time. If the cause is poor time management, the teacher could break down the assignment into smaller, more accountable steps or supervise the class more closely. If inadequate access to resources is the problem, perhaps more information is available on-site or nearby, or concurrent-assignment classes could be scheduled at different times. The teacher may have unrealistic expectations about the amount of time needed; if so, the teacher and librarian could schedule activity time more realistically. Maybe students need more time to develop production skills. Then instruction time on how to produce the product should take place upfront.

▶ WHY PARTNER?

By now, it should be obvious that no one person has all the resources or time to prepare students adequately. Nor should one. Learning is, after all, a social process. As with more personal relationships, the benefits of learning partnerships are greater than the sum of the individual contributions. Partnerships are important because students deserve the very best education possible and they need to see good models of education. In a learning community, everyone should be involved in active learning and sharing of that learning. Students need to see librarians and teachers working together so they will be motivated and equipped to work with their peers and with adults.

Certainly, teachers and librarians have needs that their counterparts can supply. Sometimes they work in parallel, each planning and implementing the same kinds of learning activities, when they could be saving time and effort by working in tandem and providing a broader base for student learning. For example, if teachers can count on librarians to instruct students in using access tools such as magazine indexes and search engines, then they can concentrate on content. If librarians can count on teachers to explain how to take notes and cite sources, then they can focus on search strategies. If technology specialists can train students in using authoring tools, then teachers and librarians can spend their time on other skills. Each educator brings a unique mix of competencies. The result is that students have a three-pronged support system to help them present content-rich, meaningful products that synthesize and demonstrate their knowledge. And in the process, educators learn from each other and develop professionally.

The following checklist details the steps in partnership negotiation:

✓ The Planning Process

In each step in partnership development, some basic questions need to be answered by the librarian and teacher.

Who is the audience? Students, teachers, parents, community?
- ☐ What are their needs in terms of information?
- ☐ What experience do they have that can help shape learning?
- ☐ What do they need to know or prepare for ahead of time?

What is the objective?
- ☐ Student learning, faculty education, public relations, fund-raising?
- ☐ What changes in behaviors or attitudes are desired?
- ☐ How will they be assessed?

What will the content be?
- ☐ What information competencies will be addressed?
- ☐ What aspects of the subject will be covered?
- ☐ What social or cooperative skills will be targeted?

What resources will be used?
- ☐ Will resources come from the library, the classroom, from students, or from outside?
- ☐ Who will supply them? Librarian, teacher, students, other agencies, other people?
- ☐ How available are they? Do students need to look off-site, or will the librarian or teacher provide them?

What delivery systems will be appropriate?
- ☐ Lecture, videotape, learning packet, Web tutorial, a combination of formats?
- ☐ Do supporting materials exist, or do they have to be produced? Who will do it?

What is the time frame?
- ☐ Is this a one-time project? If so, when should it be scheduled?
- ☐ How is it connected to other school activities?
- ☐ Will it need to be divided into smaller time periods? If so, will classes be weekly or daily?
- ☐ What follow-up time is needed?

In what location will the activity be most effectively done?
- ☐ How do the presence of other people or the facility itself (furniture, space, accessibility) affect the project?
- ☐ Where are the participants coming from, where are they going after the activity, and how will that affect the project?
- ☐ Should a combination of locations be used? Should brainstorming, research, or production occur at different sites?
- ☐ How available is the space? Are other people using it? Can it be shared?
- ☐ What seating or other furniture is needed?
- ☐ Does the area need to be rearranged?
- ☐ Is transportation a factor?
- ☐ If so, who will arrange and pay for it?
- ☐ What kind of transportation will be used? Who will drive? What insurance coverage is needed?

Who will teach or present the information?

- [ ] How will instructional duties be determined? By interest, expertise, availability?
- [ ] Will more than one person be involved?
- [ ] Will off-site people be used?
- [ ] Will they need transportation, equipment, fees?

The partners must design the learning activity.

- [ ] When and where will student practice occur?
- [ ] Will students work independently or in groups?
- [ ] Will homework be assigned?
- [ ] What standards of performance and supervision will be required?

How will the activity be evaluated?

- [ ] What will be assessed? The plan, the delivery, the activity itself, the results?
- [ ] Who will be assessed? Students, other participants, teacher, librarian?
- [ ] What assessment tools will be used? Observation, response sheets, tests, rubrics, product evaluation?
- [ ] Who will do the evaluating? Students, observers, teacher, librarian, supervisor?
- [ ] How will assessment results be used? To grade students, improve planning, improve partnerships? (More than one constituent should assess, and more than one assessment tool should be used.)

Whether the planning results in a lesson, a contest, a document, or a fund raiser, these questions provide a framework for useful discussion and implementation. Thorough planning pays dividends.

▶ WHY NOT PARTNER?

This question is as important as the previous one. If partnering is so good, why isn't everyone doing it? Prospective partners should face the complexities and challenges of partnerships with full knowledge of the consequences.

First, partnerships are not the panaceas for education. Some tasks, such as creating a bibliography or demonstrating a science experiment, really do belong to one person. Tasks like making a display or organizing a lab take so long to train others to do that it is easier and more efficient to do the task oneself. Particularly if a task is a one-time effort, such as buying shelving, partnerships are not the answer. Partnerships are for cooperative activities. A potential partnership project needs to be complex and substantial enough that it cannot be accomplished well by one person. Moreover, it should require a variety of skills. Some examples might be

- A renaissance fair,
- Schoolwide accreditation,
- Enrichment reading programs,
- Open house,
- Building campaign,
- School Web site, or
- District technology plan.

Let's face it. Partnerships are demanding, even to design:
- Finding lessons that lend themselves to collaborative planning,
- Scheduling time to operate,
- Choosing a means of instruction, and agreeing on ways to evaluate results.

Working with another person can slow one down. Particularly in higher grades, teachers may feel constrained by content demands and think that library time cuts into their teaching time. On their part, librarians may have no support staff or may be part-timers themselves. Changing tactics and developing closer professional working relationships require time and effort. The payback may be slow in coming, too long for some. What they don't see is that investing time in partnering will enable students to learn more effectively, now and for a lifetime.

Even assuming the task would benefit from partnering, such teaming won't happen if the potential partner isn't aware of the opportunity. Too often librarians complain among themselves about the difficulty of developing and maintaining effective partnerships, while classroom teachers remain woefully ignorant of the help awaiting them. Some teachers don't know or don't see the need for librarian-teacher partnerships. Few teacher credential programs include teamwork models, particularly including librarians as the collaborators. High school teachers especially tend to be credentialed in a specific subject area and consider themselves experts in their field. How could a librarian know more about their subject than they could? How could a librarian tell them how to teach their courses? A surprising number of classroom teachers don't realize that school librarians are credentialed teachers.

> A surprising number of classroom teachers don't realize that school librarians are credentialed teachers.

Librarians, too, may have been trained before partnership was emphasized. They may have been trained for another library specialty, such as public librarian. They may have been classroom teachers who wanted to escape the drudgery of grading and coursework. (Are they in for a surprise.)

Part of the problem may relate to perceptions of the library program itself. If the school community considers the library to be a warehouse of materials rather than an instructional learning center, then expectations of could be limited to acquiring, storing, and retrieving items. If administrators see the librarian as a clerk, they will not be likely to support the librarian's efforts to help develop curriculum. If, in addition, a dichotomy still exists between operations and policy-making, many librarians may be relegated to the former status. Naturally, these outdated perceptions require education on the part of the librarian.

In extreme cases, a few educators really don't *want* to partner; they may like to be autonomous; they may be burned out or fear sharing control or power. A few librarians may like just the technical part of their job. Hopefully, such people have peers to carry out partnerships.

Even if partnerships are perceived as a good thing and the library program is respected, initiating partnerships requires a proactive stance that may be intimidating for some librarians: "Who am I to tell others that they can do their job better?" "What if I'm rejected?" "How can I look credible?" Traditionally, educators have collaborated within grade level or department. Librarians may well be the first in their school to expand that approach across school lines. Some may not have the administrator's backing. Some librarians may have tried partnerships a couple of times with disappointing results and decided that partnering isn't worth the trouble. In short, educators may be fearful or uncomfortable about change in their surroundings or themselves.

In the final analysis, the entire school community needs to decide whether partnerships are in their best interest. Both short- and long-term benefits need to be identified by the school community at large. While not everyone needs to buy into the concept, strong opposition can spell disaster. Indeed, a critical mass of proponents is needed to make a significant difference.

> While not everyone needs to buy into the concept, strong opposition can spell disaster.

Moreover, the principal has to take a leadership role if partnerships are to have lasting impact. The school culture and structure need to be modified to provide

- Common time for collaboration,
- Sufficient competency or training in partnering,
- Sufficient resources,
- Opportunities for implementing plans,
- Joint assessment and accountability,
- Means to share experiences with others, and
- Recognition for collaboration.

With this kind of support, individual decisions to partner become much easier to make. Partners can focus on the task at hand rather than spend time trying to convince the powers that be of the usefulness of partnerships.

CHAPTER 3

What is a Partnership?

We can all learn from each other.
Our differences provide opportunities for greater understanding.

What are the ingredients for educational partnerships? Two parties (individual or group), a task to accomplish, a social interaction, and an environmental context. Mix those ingredients together, and what results is a power that is greater than its sum. The first step in successful partnerships is to define what a partner is and does.

▶ STARTING WITH YOURSELF

Do librarians have what it takes to collaborate with others—confidence in their own work and eagerness to share that knowledge with others for the students' sake? Fortunately, most librarians have the ability and the passion to share their expertise as well as the resources they maintain. Most of them are enthusiastic and convey that enthusiasm through a pleasant personality tempered with sensitivity. Partnership also requires a sense of respectful equality with others. Particularly since librarians are perceived as lifelong learners, they also need to convey the feeling that they are interested in what other people have to offer. Good partnerships are built on mutual encouragement and support.

Librarians also need to demonstrate trust and dependability. Part of that dependability includes acting on what one believes. Straying too far from that psychological center, perhaps because another partner is too dominant or too timid, results in inner conflict and outward dysfunction. Moreover, when inner convictions are demonstrated in long-term positive behaviors, a certain predictability ensues that helps sustain partnerships. This in tandem with expertise provides a strong foundation for lifelong collaboration throughout the school and community.

What is the typical school librarian personality? People-oriented, which facilitates initiating partnerships; intuitive, which offers insights on ways to make partnerships work; sympathetic, which helps engage and support partnerships; goal-oriented, which helps get the task done. School librarians can be seen as natural partners. Probably the greatest obstacle in developing partnerships is that others in the school community know too little about partners in general and librarians' contributions in particular. It's up to the librarian to provide the outreach and education to surmount those obstacles.

In *Type Talk at Work*, school librarian-type personalities are labeled "smooth-talking persuaders," which pretty much describes the approach needed to build partnerships in the library setting. The emphasis is on effective communication. Clarity between parties is essential. Communication needs to be open and honest. The tone needs to be professional and fair. Establishing a comfort zone allows for mutual exchange of ideas. In order to be heard and understood, the librarian also needs to be conscious of what the potential partner is doing at the time. Is he or she receptive right now? Does he need help at the start, in a crisis, during times of change? Likewise, the librarian needs to listen to the other person, getting timely feedback and acting on it.

In developing partnerships, self-knowledge is the starting point. What is important to you? Where do you act "from"? What can you contribute to a partnership? By asking yourself such questions you can center yourself, gather in your strengths, and look outward as a whole person, intellectually and emotionally. Here are some ideas for self-examination, some of which can be used to "psych out" a potential partner. When the key players in the partnership understand each other, weaknesses as well as strengths, they can avoid pitfalls and prepare for the inevitable.

ROLE-PLAY. Finish 10 sentences that start with "I am..." and rank each sentence in terms of its relative importance. Each person plays several roles in life, at different times and simultaneously. Identifying and prioritizing those roles helps the librarian determine what really matters in the grand scheme of things and forms the basis for negotiating with a partner.

TIME LINE. Create a personal time line by labeling a horizontal line by years and marking important events and partnerships along it. Use the space above and below the line to note highs and lows in life. What patterns emerge and why?

BOXES IN LIFE. Divide a sheet of paper into four parts and label them "Who I am," "Who I am not," "Who I want to be," "Who I don't want to be." This exercise helps reveal present self-concepts and future orientation. Most people have a "shadow" side that can be amazingly related to the "light" side. Both sides of the personality can be examined, harnessed, and used to approach one's potential. Knowing one's "darker" traits can help partners identify "hot buttons" that can jeopardize partnerships.

FRIEND OR FOE. List 10 people with whom you like to work. List 10 people with whom you don't like to work. What patterns emerge? If you could change one thing about each of the other people, what would it be? If you could change one thing about yourself, what would it be? This exercise not only points out the responsibility of each partner, but also identifies what factors can be controlled or not and by whom. Consider making three small changes in your library.

FOUR WAYS TO SOLVE A PROBLEM. Identify a substantial problem. Again, divide a sheet of paper into quarters. In the first section, list "What I *think* I should do." In the second, list "What I *feel* I should do." In the third, list "What I *wish* I could do." In the fourth, list "How a partner could help." Follow up with an action plan based on the answers.

▶ THE OTHER PERSON

The partner exists long before the partnership comes into being. The relationship is like a snapshot in an album or a blossom in a garden. Getting the best shot or flower requires creative use of existing conditions. Here are some questions to ask:

- What is the person's background?
- What experiences does he bring to the table?
- What skills and knowledge is the person willing to share?
- What are the person's needs and interests?
- What are the person's expectations? Are they realistic?
- What are the person's stress points?
- How does he deal with them?

Regardless of the task at hand, answering some work-related questions gives each partner clues as to how to either reinforce or complement the other for the best possible outcome.

- What is the person's learning style? Take note of Gardner's multiple intelligences.
- What is the person's processing style? Holistic or detailed, people-oriented or factual?
- What is the person's communication style? format, tone, timing, depth, objective?
- What is the person's work style? Decision-making, timing and pace, control factors, degree of autonomy and privacy, follow-through?
- To what extent is the person willing to change?
- What areas are negotiable?
- What kind of partnerships does the person prefer? Long-term vs. short, one-shot vs. continuing, process-based vs. bottom line?

By knowing these personal elements, partners can determine the working conditions that will let them get the job done most efficiently.

▶ SOCIAL INTERACTION

Partnerships are implemented social agreements, only as strong as the human connection. While partners can get a job done and not like each other, congeniality can make the work more pleasant.

In *Why Am I Afraid to Tell You Who I Am?* author John Powell defines five levels of communication.

- Level 5 is the most shallow, the kind of chatter encountered at a casual school function. It is based in manners but has little substance.
- Level 4 deals with objective facts such as announcements; personal agendas are not involved.
- Level 3 involves ideas and judgments that might be experienced at an in-service workshop. At this level, one watches others' reactions so as not to jeopardize self-esteem.
- Level 2 is gut level emotion such as might accompany an evaluation debriefing. It requires personal risk although it may not invoke change.

Level 1 is "peak" communication that leads to mutual empathy and growth. It is non-judgmental, integrates feelings and intellect, and rarely occurs in professional settings because it is usually associated with profound personal interactions. While level 1 is not a requirement for successful partnerships, the more fully partners are engaged, the better the results. Real communication, like friendship, takes time.

Normally, partnerships start off with a purpose, and each person identifies a role within that goal. A chart helps explain the process:

A PLANNING MATRIX

A table serves to graphically represent the interdependent roles of each educational player in the planning and implementation of an overarching educational program.
(CT = classroom teacher; LMT = library media teacher; TS = technology specialist; CLASS = class of students; X = major player; x = minor player)

TASK	CT	LMT	TS	CLASS
Develop Content Outcomes	X	X	x	x
Develop Social Outcomes	X			x
Develop Indicators	X	x	x	x
Develop Assessment	X	x-X	x-X	x
Develop Prerequisite Skills	X	x-X	x-X	
Diagnose Prerequisite Skills	X	x-X	x	x-X
Determine Available Resources	x-X	X	x-X	x
Determine Teaching Methodology	X	x-X	x-X	
Determine Time and Place	X	x-X	x-X	
Finalize Learning Experience	X	x	x	x
Assess Learning Experience	X	x-X	x-X	x-X

(From *More Than Information*, p. 37)

People tend to modify their behaviors in the presence of others, acting more restrained as they test the partnership waters. Over time, norms of behavior are established either formally or informally. It is usually a good idea to state these norms as guiding principles up front, so the partnership has an explicit foundation for interaction, especially if it involves a number of people. While groups usually begin politely, deferring to the head, members often become disenchanted with their leader and focus on accomplishing the task. Though it looks dysfunctional, this social dynamic actually indicates that the task at hand has precedence over individual agendas. Individuals become less restrained as they gain a group identity. In fact, if there is never any conflict, chances are that significant change is not happening.

On the other hand, an atmosphere of confrontation and distrust can undermine the goal. Here are ways to help overcome such problems:

- Clarify perceptions and establish boundaries to help identify misunderstandings.
- Listen actively, using I-messages and posing open-ended questions, to help cut tensions.

- Manage emotions and control personal responses to keep conflicts from escalating.
- Focus on individual and shared needs to balance demands and prioritize actions.

Single problems are to be solved systematically:

- Identify the problem, not just the symptoms. Validate the problem behavior.
- Determine who "owns" the problem.
- Decide whether the problem can be ignored or has to be solved.
- Brainstorm possible solutions.
- Determine consequences for each alternative.
- Choose an alternative.
- Bring the conflicted person back into the fold.
- Implement the solution, and assess its effectiveness. (Gossen)

Most people have a goal in mind when they act out. Some basic goals and reactions:

GOAL	EXAMPLE	REACTION	NEGATIVE	RESOLUTION
Attention	Clown	Annoyance	Repeat	Ignore
Power	Defy, Be stubborn	Anger	Intensify	Ask for help
Revenge	Hurt	Hurt, Retaliate	Intensify	Build trust
Inadequacy	Quit, Escape	Despair	Withdrawal	Encourage

(Dinkmeyer, 19) Once the person's social objective is determined, automatic reactions can be replaced by more effective actions that enable the group to proceed constructively.

Other negative situations may arise. Here are some ways to deal with them:

NEGATIVISM. Defuse the attitude by dividing the group into smaller units and have them discuss the issue and report out. Try to understand the reasons for the negativism; if it persists, talk with the person about those feelings.

PERSONAL ATTACK. Duck! Stay out of the middle. Know that you will survive. Get others' opinions; are perceptions shared? Ask for specific descriptions and behaviors; don't oversimplify the feelings. Listen and use the feedback.

DOMINEERING. Break the large group into smaller ones. Use fishbowl techniques. Get input on paper.

RESISTANCE. Don't force or hassle the person. Give resistance status by listening. Neutralize and convert resistance.

EXPLODING. Give the person time to cool down and regain self-control. Take him seriously. Talk with him in private.

INDECISIVE STALLING. Have the person tell what the conflict is that prevents decision. Help her solve her own problems. Push for quality and support of the group's goal. Help her make concrete action plans. Watch for anger or withdrawal.

Of course, partnerships can bring out the best in people and more options for solving conflicts as well as educational issues. The more important the task at hand and the more that partners are invested in its achievement, the more likely it is that conflicts will be overcome.

▷ THE TASK AT HAND

While it's great to be friendly, if nothing gets done, the partnership is not effective. Achievement must be the cornerstone. Ideally, the partnership should arise from the realization that the designated task requires several people's complementary talents. Such tasks might be developing standards for information literacy, developing curriculum, integrating technology, or creating cross-disciplinary activities. Once the purpose is determined, the issue is to identify which skills are needed and which people have them.

In some cases, specialized goals can complement each other.

- An entire school might develop a series of performance-based rubrics.
- Departments or grade levels might explore different aspects of reading (decoding, choice in reading, family involvement, subject-specific analysis).
- The school might coordinate student academic support: tutors, office hours, software.

Each subgroup approaches the problem from a different perspective and solves the problem differently. However, the larger goal unites their efforts. In fact, the sense of group should transcend individual identity, so when membership changes, the task itself can still progress.

Regardless of the purpose, partners need to determine the following factors:

- Ways to ensure involvement: through allocation of time, concrete benefits for constituents, meaningful division of labor;
- Means to keep partners responsible and accountable: through specific tasks with deadlines, department or grade level meeting minutes, regular newsletters;
- Methods of assessing and supporting progress: through observation, peer coaching, time line review, allocation of resources based on results; and
- Procedures for recording, managing meetings, decision-making, communicating between meetings: agendas, minutes, e-mail, listservs.

In terms of information processing, the model of knowledge management is probably the most appropriate model for school settings.

- First, information needs to be gathered, both externally in the community and internally in the school.
- Sometimes data need to be searched out using available sources (scores, lists, demographic statistics); sometimes it needs to be created through surveys or interviews. Often it needs to be filtered, extracted, or massaged to be meaningful; raw data may need to be graphed; subsets of circulation records may need to be used; standardized tests may need to be translated into another scale in order to be compared to other data.
- Then the information needs to be transformed; partners need to sort and analyze data, adding value to it by creating comparative charts, seeing patterns across disciplines, and analyzing the effects of teaching strategies on student learning results. Only then can the findings be communicated in order to inform decision-making. (*Knowledge Management*, 66-67)

If the group is dedicated to a high-stakes purpose and gets the necessary support, they can feel empowered. Particularly under tight deadlines, partners can be focused and productive. In fact, most groups tend to get 75 percent of their work done in the last 25 percent of the time. (*High Performance Teams*) They also tend to learn as they work together and may identify other people or call upon the community at large to help achieve the task.

Regardless of the extent of collaboration,

> Most groups tend to get 75 percent of their work done in the last 25 percent of the time.

certain support systems need to be in place for work to be carried out successfully. First, the group needs the freedom to work autonomously and the assurance that their work will be honored and implemented. They need adequate resources to implement the plan: a history of collaboration, an effective present-day model, a way to communicate within and across partnerships, training opportunities as needed, a means to assess progress, and a system of rewards.

The following case study exemplifies these processes:

APPLICATION FORM: 1999 GOOD IDEAS (CALIFORNIA SCHOOL LIBRARY ASSOCIATION)
Meeting Standards Via Information Literacy in the Library

BRIEF DESCRIPTION OF THE SCHOOL AND LIBRARY. Redwood is a suburban, comprehensive high school, which began implementing site-based management in 1992. It enjoys a strong scholastic record and a supportive community. As the 1994 WASC self-study indicated, the student population is becoming more diverse in terms of background and academic and social needs; about 85 percent are Caucasian (a significant portion of whom are Middle Eastern) with Latino and Afro-Americans composing a growing percentage. In addition, ESL and extensive special education services broaden the school's scope.

At this point, the library offers over 30,000 print resources and over 80 magazine subscriptions for all curricular areas, as well as a small collection of videos and audiobooks (special format for blind and disabled). Fifteen computers are networked to provide access to CD-ROMs, software and the Internet; four access the library's catalog, six support stand-alone applications, and three support special education needs. Instruction is content-embedded, and several teaching aids complement verbal help.

BRIEF DESCRIPTION OF THE PROJECT. As the school became a school reform leadership school, a focused effort was defined: assessment and means to help students meet district outcomes (reading, communication, and mathematics to begin). There was recognition of students at risk, with the intent of providing resources and services to meet their needs. The library is a vital part of that effort.

Starting with the class of 2002, students must meet a reading outcome: "Read and analyze material in a variety of disciplines." The class of 2003 must meet a technology outcome: "Use technology as a tool to access information."

Several faculty and the library staff noticed students were having problems in accessing and evaluating information. At the same time, AASL standards on information literacy were promulgated. A study group was formed, co-chaired by a science teacher and me. After extensive research, the group developed a research strategies skills inventory (their name for info literacy) aligned with AASL standards and surveyed the faculty and students as to assignments incorporating these skills (does not call for skill, assumes skill is known, teaches skill). The results were mapped for each grade as well as middle school and color-keyed by department. The entire faculty adopted the inventory and shared the responsibility for incorporating these skills throughout the curriculum. Assignments were "painted" and revised to reflect these skills.

We used several methods, from redesigning assignments, doing more instruction incorporating technology, to using more presentation formats. We also developed info literacy rubrics for process and product, teaching aids, and teacher training. As a result, students are more successful researchers, producing better projects. A greater number are meeting the reading and technology outcomes.

Feeder school library media teachers gave us feedback, and the results were shared with feeder schools who are now using these skills and products to help their students improve information literacy.

RESOURCES AND PROCESSES:

- Developed research strategies inventory based on AASL's *Information Power*, ERIC, and other sources including Colorado and Kansas studies, which were in CSLA's journal.
- Revised research handbook, including bibliographic style sheets and product/process rubric on information literacy, and teacher and student aids and made them available in print and online, even from home.
- Developed library research Web page that includes assignment-specific Web sites as well as general search engines and digital sources.
- Acquired and gave instruction on *Electric Library*.
- Library media teachers began teaching Internet searching and evaluation skills using *InfoPeople*'s (California LSTA grant) Guides.
- Developed binders on literacy, research strategies, and technology.
- Conducted two faculty in-service courses on electronic plagiarism and good Web sites (including lesson plans) using the Internet.
- Conducted workshops for feeder school faculty and LMTs using the inventory and research handbook.
- Conducted parent seminar on parent involvement and issues related to the Internet using *AmericaLinksUp* Web site.

HOW STUDENTS ACCESS, USE, AND EVALUATE INFORMATION, PROCESS, AND PRODUCT:
At this point, students access information with catalogs, indexes, and online resources (including the Internet) by using keyword and Boolean logic.

They evaluate information using rubrics, established criteria, and critical reviews. They compare similar sources for point of view, fact vs. opinion, and credibility. They also evaluate sources visually, analyze statistically, and graph information.

In manipulating information, students summarize, classify, sequence, organize graphics, outline, extract visual and numerical elements, annotate, and cite. They look for specific facts, get background information, and do in-depth research.

With their findings, students create research papers, I-search papers, brochures, critical reviews, annotated bibliographies, oral reports, skits, debates, posters, collages, visual essays, and multimedia presentations.

They evaluate their process through journal-writing, comparing themselves to a process rubric and peer review. They evaluate their product through product rubrics, peer review, and teacher assessment.

PROJECT COLLABORATORS AND THEIR ROLES IN CO-PLANNING, CO-IMPLEMENTATION, AND CO-EVALUATION: A science teacher and I co-chaired the Research Strategies Study Group for a semester and had weekly meetings with department representatives. The second semester I had a social studies teacher co-chair with the science teacher, and I was the main support person (to broaden leadership in the process). The three of us took the lead in creating the inventory and revising the research handbook. The larger study group committee "massaged" the inventory and surveyed their constituents. Several classroom teachers piloted the handbook and fine-tuned it. I spearheaded the process rubric with their input, and the science teacher worked with the rubrics committee to polish the product rubric.

I took the lead working with feeder schools and parents, and the two classroom teachers led two faculty in-service courses. I worked with the computer literacy teachers, so I could teach their students how to search on the Net and evaluate sources. (I also assessed their students' work.) The computer specialist and I created the library research Web page, and teachers provided me with additional Web sites, which I added to the page. (At a faculty in-service, all participants evaluated the existing Web page and sites and made suggestions for expansion.)

All of the faculty responded to the inventory, discussed its implications, adopted it, and wove it into their curriculum. Department heads and I evaluated their assignments in light of information literacy, and they redesigned those activities in light of the inventory and in-service insights. Besides our own evaluation of the project, the school's site council evaluated the research handbook and the group's project. Parents and faculty also evaluated their workshops.

ADDITIONAL INFORMATION ABOUT THE PROJECT:
When I started at Redwood five years ago, I proposed a scope-and-sequence of information literacy skills which was passively adopted and then ignored. The reason this project was so effective was that

1. It grew out of teacher-perceived need,
2. The effort was student-centered,
3. Classroom teachers partnered with me, taking leadership responsibility for the product and impact, and
4. The entire faculty was involved throughout the process and owned it. Departments took the lead in examining their practice and improving it; in the process, I worked more closely with them than ever before.

The fact that this project responded to a schoolwide reform effort and district outcomes gave it impetus and administrative support (including a period off for the co-chair). The high profile of rubrics in the school made it easier to construct and use them. Having national AASL standards and research studies on hand gave the project credibility. Creating a simple-to-use Web research page with quick updates has broadened access to research sources at both school and home.

In the process, I negotiated much more than usual. If faculty wanted to use the term "research strategies," I went along with it. They needed in-service courses on plagiarism, so I emphasized that aspect more than I would have independently. In short, I think I was sensitive to the community's needs and comfort zones and worked with them so they would own the results and use them to help students become information literate.

The incorporation of technology has also strengthened faculty interest in improving their skills and integrating it into their classroom. More multimedia projects are being developed, and the school is now poised to develop a Digital High School proposal.

▶ INDIVIDUALS VS. GROUPS

Partnerships can exist between two individuals, an individual and a group, or two groups. Each configuration has different parameters and outcomes.

The core of *one-to-one partnerships* is reciprocity: mutual support and responsibility. The classic two-person partnership is classroom teacher and librarian. The classic task is a subject-based research project. With this arrangement, tasks can be quickly identified and delegated. Typically, this kind of partnership is closer than other kinds because the partners are interdependent. Issues are obvious and must be dealt with upfront.

Another typical partnership for librarians is *individual and group,* such as a department. Usually, this kind of partnership arises out of specific need. Either the department needs a library service (such as a list of historical novels and strategies to incorporate them into the curriculum) or the librarian needs help from the department (such as incorporating information literacy instruction into a subject area). The trick is to develop a level playing field. The first step is to establish a professional relationship that benefits both sides. For example, the librarian will create a course-specific bibliography *if* the affected teachers will plan the curriculum collaboratively with the librarian. At that point, equal efforts and gains are of paramount importance.

Eventually, though, the partnership can become a unit, with the librarian considered part of the department. A sense of belonging evolves, extending into the social realm as well as the academic. This development typically takes a long-term commitment and a history of successful partnership activities. The fast track to this stage is mentorship by a respected, powerful person in the department who can ease the way and give the librarian inside information about department personalities and norms. There is a cost for this service: loyalty to the mentor. Therefore, it is wise to check out the credibility of the mentor ahead of time and determine whether the fit is good. This variation of the individual-group partnership is actually a one-to-one partnership within a larger context. Difficulty arises if the mentor partnership changes. Adjusting to that change can be uncomfortable. The collaborative level of the rest of the department will, in the final analysis, determine how easy it is to maintain the group partnership absent the mentor.

A third partnership is composed of *two groups working together.* The groups usually consist of departments, grade levels, or the faculty in partnership with parents or students. Usually the broader the group or the more heterogeneous the group identity, the weaker the partnership, because it is difficult to do in-depth, coordinated work en masse. Sometimes the librarian's group consists of the library staff of professionals, paraprofessionals and volunteers; sometimes library staff consists of one person, not a group.

But librarians may join other local librarians in school or non-school settings. They may belong to a group like AAUW (American Association of University Women), a youth organization such as Girl Scouts, PTSA (as a staff person or a parent), a local service club such as Rotary, or a religious organization. Sometimes librarians assume "librarian-like" positions within those groups, acting as archivist or Webmaster, or contribute other talents like pho-

> Usually the broader the group or the more heterogeneous the group identity, the weaker the partnership, because it is difficult to do in-depth, coordinated work en masse.

tography or singing. These "outside" activities enhance the librarian's role as a partner; he is seen as a well-rounded individual.

No matter the group configuration, the librarian needs to be aware of group norms and act within them, believing in the group and its aims. The benefit of group affiliation is strength in numbers; powerful outcomes can be realized. Passing major legislation, creating whole-school reform, and developing statewide information literacy standards are just a few of the possibilities that rise from multi-group collaboration.

A district-wide library plan demonstrates the impact of partnerships among groups:

 District Library Plan

DISTRICT MISSION. To graduate students with the skills and desires to become lifelong learners. We will accomplish this goal by involving staff, students, parents, and community in a dynamic and comprehensive teaching and learning process that helps all students achieve their potential in a caring environment. We will operate with place the highest importance on our students' education and their needs.

DISTRICT LIBRARY PROGRAM MISSION. In support of this goal, the district's library program has as its mission to ensure that students and staff are effective users of ideas and information. This mission is accomplished by
- Providing intellectual and physical access to materials in various formats,
- Providing instruction to foster competence and stimulate interest in reading, viewing, and using information and ideas, and
- Working with other educators to design learning strategies to meet the needs of individual students.

DISTRICT LIBRARY NEEDS. In assessing the needs of the district (following state Department of Education's *Check It Out!* guidelines), these areas were found to be critical:
- An explicit district policy for ensuring equitable access to library resources,
- Regular evaluation of district library service programs,
- Improved communications among sites, particularly with alternative schools, and
- Improved library collections through site-based plans.

These areas for improvement form the basis for the goals of this three-year library plan.

LIBRARY PLAN ADMINISTRATION. In examining district operations, it was determined that library planning and improvement needs to be site-based as much as possible to address specific school community needs. Thus, the district administrative model delegates must work to the sites, with the district library steering committee acting as the coordinating body.
- A district library steering committee composed of the library media teachers, a San Andreas representative, a Tamiscal representative, and the assistant superintendent for instruction will act as the operating committee to advise and review district efforts. They will review and

revise the district library plan yearly and will report to the district board of trustees.
- Site-based committees composed of the library media teacher, faculty, students, parents, and administrator will provide the main planning and implementation leadership for each school. They will report to the district library steering committee.

LIBRARY ACTION PLAN

Goal 1: To develop a district policy for ensuring equitable access to library resources.

Strategy:

1. Library media teachers (LMTs) will select existing policies about equitable access.
2. Assistant Superintendent Christine Anderson will draft the district policy using existing policies as guides.
3. The district library planning steering committee (DLSC) will review and finalize the policy for recommendation to the board of trustees.
4. The district school board will approve the new policy in January.

Goal 2: To evaluate district library service programs.

Strategy:

1. LMTs will select and develop standards and assessment tools to measure library service programs (i.e., library improvement plan). They will ensure that external standards, such as WASC, will be incorporated into the assessment.
2. DLSC will review the assessment tools by March.
3. Site committees will review their library service programs in spring.
4. DLSC will review the programs' assessments, update the library plan with recommended action plans based on the findings and report to the district board of trustees.
5. Subsequently, library service programs will be evaluated yearly.

Goal 3: To improve communications among sites, particularly with alternative schools.

1. All sites will be represented on the DLSC.
2. All sites will communicate among themselves about new library resources and current services.
3. LMTs will coordinate resource-sharing as appropriate.
4. The alternative schools will have electronic access to Redwood's library catalog and to *Electric Library* by January.
5. DLSC will evaluate communications in terms of timeliness, regularity, and response (greater library use, greater circulation of library materials, more instruction and teacher collaboration).

Goal 4: To improve site library collections.

1. All sites will establish or update a site-based library plan to allocate AB862 funds by February.
2. The DLSC will review the site library plans by February.
3. LMTs will order resources, based on site plans, by March.
4. The site committees and DLSC will report to the state department of education in October about AB862 allocations.
5. LMTs will evaluate the sites' library collections as part of the library service program evaluation process.

SUPPORTING DOCUMENTS:

Check it Out! California State Department of Education, 1998

Information Power. American Library Association, 1998

Loertscher, D. *Reinvent Your School's Library.* Willow Press, 1998

(From Tamalpais Union High School District, California)

▶ VIRTUAL PARTNERS

With telecommunications, partnerships can go global. As long as there is a common goal based on a compelling need and committed, resourceful people to achieve those goals, much of the communication effort can occur in cyberspace. (Note: the *real* work still needs to be actual and hands-on. It takes real money, time, and sweat to produce results.) One of the main advantages of virtual partners, besides the short commute to the computer, is the notion of asynchronous collaboration: Partners don't have to meet at the same time to brainstorm or exchange ideas. E-mail is the classic means to share ideas any time.

Of course, if real time communication is vital, chat rooms (using *First Class* software, for instance) and video conferencing (*CUSeeMe* is a low-end software solution) can shrink the planet to the size of two workstations. When the technology allows partners to analyze and modify the same documents simultaneously with electronic whiteboards or groupware such as *Lotus: Notes*, the collaboration is highly effective.

Some factors optimize these virtual partnerships:

- Virtual "introductions" so each partner has some idea of the person on the other end of the line;
- Regular communication, at least weekly;
- A tight focus based on a concrete need;
- Concrete tasks that can be done between communication connection time;
- Systems of responsibility and accountability;
- Advance notice if real-time conversation is being scheduled; and
- A means to archive all communication for possible threading and permanent documentation.

Telecommunication makes it possible to enlist the key people needed to achieve an important goal, even though they are located halfway across the state or country, rather than settle for less than the best brains.

Here is an example of a telecommunications-based collaboration between a middle school class and a high school class:

INTERNET TEAM PROJECT
Growing up in Time

ACTIVITY DESCRIPTION. Middle school and high school classes cooperatively produce a Web page about being a child or young adult during a period in American history.

CONTENT OUTCOMES. Students will

- Identify events, daily life, politics, demographics, and other characteristics of an American historical period.
- Accurately describe being a child or young adult during an American historical period.
- Compare conditions between age groups and historical periods.

INFORMATION LITERACY OUTCOMES. Students will

- Recognize and use a variety of sources, especially primary sources from LC's *American Memory* collection of information about youth in specific periods of American history.
- Assess information from a variety of sources to verify facts, recognize

perspectives, and determine adequacy of information.
- Synthesize and organize findings into Web page format.

RATIONALE FOR THE PROCESS. Growing up is an immediate issue for youth. Comparing today's conditions with those of other historical periods in America helps students learn to crystallize and humanize facts. By creating Web pages, students share their findings with their counterparts and learn from each other.

RESOURCES:
- *American Memory* collection (Revolutionary era broadsides, Civil War photos, African American pamphlets, urban American visuals, Depression oral histories);
- Other online primary sources such as UC Berkeley's digital library, University of Virginia's primary sources;
- *American Heritage* articles,
- Monographs of each period,
- Local history collections,
- Web authoring tools, scanners, DTP

GROUPING: Small heterogeneous cooperative groups. Middle schoolers will research being a child, while high schoolers will research being a young adult.

GROUP TASKS:
1. Choose a period in American history.
2. Locate and select information, especially primary sources, about being a child or young adult during that period.
3. Determine one demographic feature, one socioeconomic situation, or region for each student to use to focus and differentiate his or her research.
4. Based on the analysis of information, publish a visual and textual description of the youths' lifestyle on a Web page.
5. High school students will compare the living conditions of children and young adults based on the middle and high school Web pages.

TIPS: Introduce the activity by leading a class discussion about growing up now, asking questions such as
- What distinguishes today's youth?
- What issues do youth have to deal with?
- How do socioeconomic conditions influence growing up?
- How might the historical period affect youth development?

Remind groups to search for information from various angles: by ethnic groups, time, region, gender roles, family, daily life. Explain how details can make the description more effective by discussing a typical day and its factors: food, transportation, clothing, home life, money. This will help students ferret out interesting aspects of the period. Groups should also use a variety of information formats: eyewitness accounts, film documentaries, oral histories, illustrations.

ASSESSMENT. Each group publishes a Web page, which is evaluated by their partner-school counterparts. Criteria will include accuracy, thoroughness, appearance, and technical skill. Classes discuss growing up in different historical periods, comparing socioeconomic conditions.

Who is a Partner?

No one can do everything, but everyone can do something. Snowflakes are one of nature's most fragile things, but just look at what they can do when they stick together.

The entire school community is composed of potential partners, each with a unique set of characteristics, abilities, needs, and expectations. Staff members often duplicate each other's work, each planning and implementing activities that could be accomplished more effectively in tandem. The duplication may be as general as two groups promoting outside reading for the same students or as specific as two different teachers showing the same students how to evaluate Web sites.

It's a given that everyone wants to help students. It's also a given that each has limited time and resources. Together, school community members can complement and supplement each other's efforts. If the history teacher knows that the English teacher has explained bibliographic citations, social studies classes can concentrate on comparing primary and secondary sources. If the science teacher knows that the school librarian will instruct students on ways to find relevant magazine articles, he can spend more time in biology linking current events to scientific principles. If parents read aloud to their children, classroom teachers can build on that practice at storytime. Everyone benefits.

▶ CLASSROOM TEACHERS

The most obvious partner is the teacher, the organizer and evaluator of most student learning experiences. Teachers possess content knowledge about their academic discipline or psychological knowledge about a specific age group. They also know how to teach the processes that undergird such knowledge. Teachers also have personal knowledge about their students, especially if they teach one group all day, every day. Because of their in-depth contact with students, teachers are probably the most directly influential group of adults in schools. Librarians do well to work through teachers to reach students efficiently to promote information literacy and reading support, for instance.

Of course, librarians need to meet teachers' expectations. What do teachers want? The best for their students: the best resources, facilities conducive to learning, instruction, encouragement, and assistance as needed. Does the library provide physical and intellectual access to the materials needed to accomplish the assignment? Does the library have areas for student research, collaboration, production? Does the library have signage and other learning aids to help students locate and evaluate information? Is library instruction effective and followed up with individualized and responsive student coaching? As librarians provide services to teachers, they demonstrate concern. This outgoing approach helps lay the foundation for mutual gain.

Certainly, librarian-teacher partnerships imply two-way benefits. The greater the communication and planning together, the more prepared both librarians and teachers will be to help students. The more the collection is developed collaboratively, the more likely that library resources (including access to virtual sources) will meet curricular needs. Just as the library can reinforce thematic units in classes, so too can classes support library events such as Teen Read Week.

What are some factors that librarians should heed when working with teachers? That teachers work on two levels: the ideal long-term and the practical short-term (maybe the next hour). A solid partnership aids both modes because it provides a consistent foundation for courses and is flexible enough to allow for short-term changes. Particularly since actual lesson plans seldom occur in strict sequential order; if the librarian can enter at any point in the planning cycle he is more likely to be able to handle challenges as they occur and ensure that students get the information literacy skills they need. And the more often that the librarian and teacher work together, the more likely they will understand each other's favored style of planning and instructing as well as their long-term objectives.

> **Making appropriate accommodations as the situation demands can result in a strong if somewhat "fuzzy" partnership.**

In fact, planning may take on an organic "presence" rather than a formal written list of objectives, resources, and delivery systems. If the librarian can tolerate some ambiguity, making appropriate accommodations as the situation demands can result in a strong if somewhat "fuzzy" partnership. And each person's style may well "rub off" onto the other, broadening the educational repertoire of each.

Here are some starting points for teacher-librarian discussion:

TEACHER PLANNING TIPS FOR STUDENT SUCCESS IN THE LIBRARY

The more you plan your unit in partnership with the librarian, the more successful your students will be and the happier you will be. The more complete the details, the more that can be worked out to everyone's satisfaction. It's great to brainstorm with another professional, too.

KNOW YOUR SCHEDULE:

- Sign up for optimum days. Teachers can sign up for a half-period to give more access to other classes.
- Sign up half a class for those students needing extra time.
- Check with the librarian to see if other classes are working on similar topics.
- If you need to cancel or reschedule a class, contact the librarian immediately so other classes can be scheduled. (This works to everyone's advantage; you may have a last-minute need to use the library.)

KNOW YOUR OBJECTIVES:

- Is it to access information? The librarian can give a mini-lecture to start students out or produce a "pathway" page or bookmark Web sites to guide students to resources.
- Is it to evaluate information? The librarian can locate sources and create a reserve shelf or cart of items. He can instruct students on evaluation techniques or provide evaluation guide sheets.
- Is it to find specific facts? Reference materials will be most useful. The librarian can develop a clippings file to collect hard-to-find specifics.
- Is it to make inferences from primary and narrative sources? Books in the general collection and digital sources will be most useful. (*Note:* Consider fictional works to provide a sociological perspective on issues.)

KNOW YOUR TOPIC:

- Does the assignment have one topic? Check with the librarian to see if enough material exists. Pin down the topic so the library staff and students understand the parameters. Develop options or subtopics so students will have several places to find information.
- Does the assignment include several topics? Check with the librarian to see if enough material exists. Rework topics or develop other topics based on available resources, in partnership with the librarian.

KNOW YOUR SOURCES:

- What is accessible from the library? The teacher and librarian can browse the collection and the Internet for sources.
- Can materials be brought in? With prior notice, the librarian can get sources from other sites or buy needed sources.

KNOW WHAT CIRCULATION POLICIES EXIST:

- Are many students using a limited number of sources? The librarian can create a reserve shelf or cart. Books can be checked out overnight, for three days, or they can stay in the library.
- Are several classes doing the same project? The librarian can create a reserve shelf or cart. Sources can stay in the library until the last day of class research time. Classes can be rescheduled to ensure greater access to needed sources.

▶ SUPPORT STAFF

Increasingly, technology specialists and paraprofessionals work with librarians to maintain a working learning environment. Like teachers, support staff have subject expertise, both in content and process. Support staff may be viewed as problem-oriented personnel. Here are some scenarios:

- Technology specialists troubleshoot computer problems and help others learn how to take advantage of a variety of resource formats.
- Counselors help solve students' academic and personal problems.
- Nurses address physical and sometimes psychological needs.
- Secretaries and other office workers typically take care of document and procedural issues.
- Maintenance personnel manage facilities issues.
- Food services satisfy nutritional needs.

Partnerships between support personnel and librarians can be mutually beneficial. For instance:

- Technology specialists help maintain library equipment. Particularly when libraries network with the rest of the school; technological expertise relieves librarians of many hours of work so they can concentrate on resource deployment and instruction. On the other hand, librarians can test potential software or read reviews to determine their educational appropriateness. Librarians can also order sound technology manuals and locate useful Web-based technology tutorials.
- Counselors can offer insights about students and suggest good candidates as library aides. They may also discover collection gaps or notify the librarian about students' personal issues. At times, counselors also provide an ear for librarians' own concerns. In response, librarians can suggest therapeutic books, parenting materials, and resources to support counseling efforts.
- Nurses may suggest good sources on health and fitness that librarians can acquire for the good of the entire school community.
- Office personnel can help smooth bureaucratic pathways for librarians. Librarians, on their part, can offer organizational and technological expertise.
- Maintenance workers help make the library a livable environment. Librarians can research recycling options and find MSDS information.
- Food services can cater library events. In return, librarians can research novel recipes for international food fairs.

> **Support staff may be viewed as problem-oriented personnel.**

In each case, the more that support staff and librarians understand each other's contributions and needs, the more they can benefit each other and their clientele. This form demonstrates one means towards clearer communication and more satisfactory results:

SAMPLE EQUIPMENT PROGRAM REPORT FORM

Name: _____ Room: _____ Date: _____

Station number (if applicable):

DID YOU CHECK THE FOLLOWING:

☐ Is the electricity working (outlet, switch, power strip)?

☐ Is it plugged in?

☐ Are all the connections secure?

☐ Is it turned on?

FOR PRINTERS:

☐ Is there paper?

☐ Is there enough ink (toner, cartridge, ribbon)?

☐ Is the right printer selected on the computer system?

SYSTEM QUESTIONS:

☐ Is the problem local to one machine?

☐ Is the problem consistent or is it intermittent?

☐ Does the problem exist for all software resources or just one?

EQUIPMENT:

Type of machine: Brand: Model:

Part of machine having trouble:

DESCRIPTION OF PROBLEM:

When did it happen?

What happened at the time that the problem occurred?

What does the problem look like?

What did you do to correct the problem? What happened?

How urgent is the problem?

ACTION:

Date and time form received:

Who fixed problem: Date and time fixed:

Solution:

(From *Training Student Library Staff,* p. 113)

▶ ADMINISTRATORS

Principals set the tone for the school community, influencing the potential success of all members. Particularly with whole-school reform and site-based management, the principal acts as the instructional visionary and agent for cohesive change. Certainly, good relationships with administrators underlie effective library service and promote partnerships with other parts of the school community.

In the grand scheme of things, though, the principal may underestimate the partnership potentials of the librarian. Few administration preparation courses include information about library services, and if the library is operating efficiently, the principal may overlook it. Thus, the librarian needs to educate administrators, in line with their style and needs. *Information Power* is a good place to start, particularly if it can be aligned with site efforts.

On their part, librarians may not realize the complexities of administration, although more and more librarians are getting administrative credentials. Here are basic administrative skills paired with the librarian's roles:

- Educational leadership; spearheading educational technology reform
- Implementing educational programs; coordinating information literacy instruction
- Management of educational personnel; training and supervising volunteer and paid staff
- School-community relations; developing an adopt-a-book program
- Legal and financial; inservice training on copyright issues
- Educational governance and politics; serving on site council
- School management; mentoring beginning teachers
- Mainstreaming; providing adaptive technology

On their part, administrators need to be effective users of information and partners with librarians. The American Association of School Librarians developed a set of these competencies for beginning administrators:

- Supporting the incorporation of information literacy across the curriculum: model information literacy, hold teachers accountable for information literacy, comply with legal access to information.
- Supporting resource-based learning: provide resources, money, and time for teachers.
- Using literature for learning: model reading, expect teachers to offer reading experiences.
- Using technology as a resource tool: use online resources, support staff development; assess teacher use of technology.
- Partnering: support teacher collaboration through scheduling and budgeting, involve staff in governance.

> **Principals set the tone for the school community, influencing the potential success of all members.**

Librarians can also further administrative agendas by providing background research for schoolwide projects, locating potential grant sources, and teaching technology skills. While the librarian should not be the teacher "spy," he can act as a cross-curricular mentor.

As leaders and supporters of academic programs, administrators can clear the way for new courses. On their part, librarians can provide the setting and resources to make that service happen. Here is a course of study in support of such a goal:

TAs IN TECHNOLOGY
Course of Study In-School Work Experience

BACKGROUND: This course is a specialty within the board-approved course of study for in-school work experience. It conforms to credit limits, general objectives and course content, and placement procedures. This document details the placement, content, delivery system, and assessment for the program.

CREDIT LIMITS: Exploratory work experience may earn up to 20 units of credit.

OBJECTIVES:
- Explore school-related occupations.
- Learn to use and care for equipment and applications for computer workstations.
- Further develop occupational skills related to course.
- Develop acceptable and desirable work habits.

PLACEMENT PROCEDURES:
1. Student plans program with counselor based on needs, interests, and capabilities.
2. Student completes Work Experience/School Service form and application (including letter of recommendation from teacher or other adult who knows the student's skills and dependability) and submits them to supervising teacher.
3. The teacher interviews the applicant and consults with the counselor in terms of appropriate work assignments and periods.
4. If the job is mutually acceptable, a program change slip is submitted, and the student begins work.

TECH TEAM (TA) ROLES: Technology TAs (Tech Team) have the generic role of facilitating the use of technology within the school. They work under the direction of the educational computer specialist or other faculty member (library media teacher). (The term "Tech Team" may designate those students working under the supervision of the computer specialist.) Tech TAs may work in several capacities:
- Lab assistant
- Trainer or coach for students and teachers (application use)
- Systems specialist (installation, troubleshooting, cleaning)
- Clerical help (inventory, record-keeping)
- Product developer (create instructional aids for teachers)

Each Tech TA should have the opportunity to carve out an individual niche for teaching and learning as long as it is aligned with the school's needs and resources.

SKILLS: There are two Tech Team levels: apprentice and journeyman. First year Tech Team members are apprentices who start by shadowing a Tech Team journeyman or supervising adult. Journeyman Tech Team members teach skills to peers and learn additional skills. Apprentices should be at least sophomores; journeymen should be at least juniors with one year's experience as an apprentice. All Tech TAs must perform at a basic or higher level of technical skill.

Those skills include:
- The ability to pass computer literacy competency and ethical use assessment, and
- Basic use of the Internet.

The following types of work experience involve unique skills beyond these basics for which the student should exhibit a desire to learn.

LAB ASSISTANT:
- Word processing
- Additional applications (may be subject-specific such as science)
- Lab procedures
- Basic operating systems
- Teaching or tutoring
- Interpersonal, patience

TRAINER OR COACH (FOR STUDENTS AND TEACHERS):
- Advanced competence in applications (may be subject-specific)
- Teaching or tutoring
- Interpersonal, patience

SYSTEMS SPECIALIST:
- Software installation
- Advanced operating systems (may specialize)
- Troubleshooting
- Equipment maintenance

CLERICAL:
- Database and spreadsheet
- Word processing
- Attention to detail

PRODUCT DEVELOPER:
- Advanced competence in applications (may specialize)
- Programming (optional)
- Interface design
- Design brief
- Word processing
- Graphics
- Communications
- HTML
- Interpersonal

ASSESSMENT: Authentic assessment (how well the student performs) is the basis for grading. Specific criteria: degree and quality of competency, self-direction, cooperation, dependability, and responsibility.

STUDENT CONTRACT:

Name: _____ Student ID#: _____

Grade: _____ Homeroom Teacher: _____

I want to become a Tech Team member because:

I am applying to work in the following capacities (check as many as are relevant):

☐ Lab assistant ☐ Trainer or coach ☐ Systems specialist (install/troubleshoot/clean)
☐ Clerical assistant ☐ Product developer (create instructional aids for teachers)

My technology experience and skills include:

My educational objectives as a Tech Team member are (skills and products):

My plan for achieving my objectives is:

The evidence to assess how well I achieve my objectives will be:

Other comments: (language ability, constraints)

I agree to the terms of this contract: Semester/year:

Student: Date:

Teacher: Date:

(From Tamalpais Union High School District, California)

▶ STUDENTS

Students today have greater voice and responsibility for their learning. They bring their personal experiences and interests to the table, which librarians can tap into as they explore information together. In partnership with librarians, students can get the most out of their educational opportunities.

The entire learning process lends itself to student-librarian interaction. When students choose meaningful questions to investigate within the scope of information literacy skills, the librarian can help craft or frame those queries to optimize the chances for success. Librarians help students learn effective search strategies and evaluation methods and bookmark worthwhile URLs for class assignments. On their part, students can help librarians fill collection gaps and suggest appealing resources. Librarians and students can help each other with production techniques and skills; they can cooperatively design Web tutorials on Internet skills. Librarians can help students find forums for expression by providing cyberspace for student Web pages, shelf space for publications, broadcast time for videotapes, and display space for artwork.

In addition, students help carry out the library program's mission in several ways as
- Advocates for the library program,
- Reviewers,
- Technical assistants,
- Peer tutors, and
- Program or event planners.

One particularly satisfying partnership is tutoring service provided by students in the library:

TUTORING TECHNIQUES

OBJECTIVE: The tutor will use techniques that teach information literacy.

PROCESS: The trainer will demonstrate effective tutoring techniques, help the trainee determine the critical features of effective tutoring, and coach the trainee as he practices tutoring others.

DEMONSTRATION IDEAS:
- Videotape effective tutoring practices and analyze the process.
- Have a professional tutor demonstrate effective techniques and practices.
- Discuss the trainee's experiences in being tutored or coached.
- Develop a list of effective and ineffective techniques.

LEARNING ACTIVITIES: Have the trainee
- Train another library staff member.
- Critique another person's tutoring techniques.
- Interview tutors and learners in terms of effective techniques.
- Write directions for a library task.

FOLLOW-UP: Discuss the relationship of tutoring to large group discussion. Compare tutoring with self-guided instruction. Discuss the significance of interpersonal skills in successful tutoring.

ASSESSMENT: Does the trainee
- Communicate articulately with the person being tutored?

TUTORING TECHNIQUES cont.

- Explain the skill or process clearly and accurately?
- Practice good interpersonal skills?
- Train the learner to accomplish the task or apply the concept effectively and independently?

STEPS IN BECOMING AN EFFECTIVE LIBRARY TUTOR:

1. Clarify what the person wants to learn.
2. Agree on what you will teach.
3. Agree on the length of time.
4. Find an appropriate place to tutor.
5. Have all materials and resources available.
6. Find out what the person already knows.
7. Explain one concept at a time. Define all unknown terms.
8. Demonstrate or model the skill.
9. Walk through the process one step at a time. Check to make sure the person understands before continuing to the next step.
10. Have the person explain the concept. Correct as needed.
11. Have the person go through the process. Correct as needed.
13. Have the person practice the skill, allowing them to ask for help as needed.
14. Ask the person if he needs any more help. Repeat steps as needed.
15. Thank the person and leave him to work independently.

GENERAL HINTS:

- Be professional: be friendly, respectful and helpful.
- Communicate effectively: be clear and articulate, be heard, and be thorough.
- Listen attentively and respond appropriately.
- Be patient and keep a sense of humor.

ESTABLISHING A TUTORING PROGRAM:

1. Train a number of people as tutors. Certify them for specific areas of expertise: reading, Internet searching, research strategies, content specialist. Make a certified tutor card from half an index card for each person.
2. Develop a database of tutors. Using the following fields, the database can be sorted by specialty and availability:
   Name   *Specialties*
   Availability *Sign-up*
3. Post the database. Faculty and students can sign up for tutoring or simply ask the tutor if he is available for quick help. If the posted list is laminated, scheduling can be done with a wipe-off marker each day or week. If installed on a Web page, it can be updated frequently.
4. Encourage students to assess their tutors.
5. Provide opportunities for tutors to improve their skills. Have weekly debriefing meetings, or use a tutor notebook to jot down successes and needs.
6. Recognize good work.

(From *Training Student Library Staff*, p. 159-160)

▶ PARENTS AND GUARDIANS

Students' first teachers are their parents or guardians. Even though teenagers may assume major responsibility for their learning, their parents still provide an educational safety net and remain the main experts about their children. Librarian partnerships with parents not only help the children but foster a positive, supportive learning environment schoolwide and, in particular, advance the library's mission.

Parents may be involved at different levels as library partners. At the most basic level, parents want to do a good job raising their children. Librarians can work with parents by providing parenting resources, training parents in technology, and suggesting ways to encourage and reinforce reading at home.

At the next level, parents want to communicate with the school, so librarians need to make sure that there is a library presence in school publications to students' homes as well as on school Web pages accessed from their homes.

On a higher level, parents become involved in school governance and advocacy issues. That is where a Friends of the Library group comes into play and when parent volunteers really make a difference. At this point, the librarian can introduce parents to the school network and offer them background research on topics of concern.

At the highest level, parents want to help improve school programs systematically and link schools with the community at large. These folks constitute the parent part of the library council, pushing for greater library staffing and services. The librarian can work with council members to create and administer school grants.

Regardless of their level of participation, parents want to help in order to help their children, gain status or work experience, gain a sense of belonging, or feel that they are contributing to the greater good. In order to foster their involvement in the library, librarians need to address issues of transportation, child care, cultural differences, social acceptance, and recognition. On a social level, librarians need to acknowledge parental expertise and empower them to help guide others.

Fortunately, there are many ways that parents can help at all levels:

- Library advocacy,
- Program and event planning,
- Tutoring,
- Storytelling,
- Communications: publications, speaking, telecommunications, and
- Fund-raising

Note that parents are natural volunteers and can assume many library functions such as processing, shelving, and display work, but their chief strength lies in their ability to work as advocates to advance the library program.

One aspect of the parental partnership that is often overlooked is their role on school boards. Particularly since this group of people determines much of the local policy, librarians need to educate school boards about the current library program and to involve them on an ongoing basis to develop long-term partnerships. Librarians can show boards how library services impact student learning in theory and in local practice. On a personal level, librarians can research educational issues for board members. When library policies such as Internet access need to be updated, having an established relationship with the board will help bring about needed changes. And by keeping the board in mind, the librarian will have an easier time getting proposals and grant applications approved by this vital governing force.

Several examples of opportunities for parent partnership are

FRIENDS OF THE LIBRARY FLYER

Make the Library Connection Better
Survey for Friends of the Library

Announcing something <u>very special</u> for our school: a stronger support organization

BACKGROUND: Redwood High School Library has been an active hub of learning since its opening in 1958. It continues to add resources and space, largely with the help of friends like you.

TODAY: We have a vision for enriching the library, the students, and the lives of the community through expansion of a committee of parents, staff, alumni, and friends. We call them Friends of the Library. We ask your help with ideas, a sense of your interest, and encouragement in whatever ways you can give.

PLEASE COMPLETE THIS SURVEY BELOW TO HELP US WITH PLANNING.

1. How would you like to participate in Friends of the Library?
- ☐ As a working committee member for fundraising and resources donations
- ☐ As a social planner to develop receptions, concerts and special events
- ☐ As a book discussion participant or organizer
- ☐ As a volunteer to help operate the library
- ☐ As an advocate to foster library awareness
- ☐ Other:

2. What kinds of activities do you think appropriate for members?
- ☐ Newsletter
- ☐ Use of library facilities
- ☐ Gifts such as bookplates
- ☐ Personal recognition
- ☐ Social receptions
- ☐ Other:

3. What level of annual membership fee would you find comfortable?
- ☐ $25   ☐ $15   ☐ $10
- ☐ $50   ☐ Other:

Want to become active? Please complete the section below and return it to the library.

- ☐ Yes, I'd like to help. Contact me.
- ☐ Yes, keep me informed of your progress, and put me on your mailing list.
- ☐ Yes, I would like to:
    - ☐ donate time
    - ☐ donate resources
    - ☐ help raise funds
    - ☐ participate in events
    - ☐ other:

NAME:

ADDRESS:

TELEPHONE: E-MAIL:

Announcing...

a valuable program that's fun for your child and you... and helps our library add new books, magazines, and software. It's called **ADOPT-A-BOOK**.

"Next to acquiring good friends, the best acquisition is that of good books." — Colton

Your child deserves the best in education. Our school supports your child's learning through caring teachers and challenging curricula.

You may ask, "How may I help my son or daughter become a better student?" One answer is to provide high-quality information resources. Good books, magazines, and software need to be available in abundance to answer your student's questions.

Right now our library offers a broad and cost-effective means for your student to acquire and use these resources. But the library needs your partnership.

Our library is starting the Adopt-a-Book program. If you decide to adopt a book or magazine, a special bookplate will be placed in the resource that the library media teacher buys for the collection. You will receive "adoption papers" for the item and a donation statement for your records.

Your "adoptee" will have a happy home in our library, to be enjoyed by many students. And, of course, you have visiting rights!

If you choose to adopt now, please complete the return the attached form. The school and the students thank you for your support.

Student's name: _____

I want to adopt as indicated below (please choose a resource in the following areas):

☐ Fiction book: ☐ Reference book: ☐ Software:
☐ Nonfiction book: ☐ Magazine:
☐ I would like this specific title: _____

To this end, I wish to donate

☐ $25   ☐ $10   ☐ $35   ☐ $50   ☐ $100   ☐ $:

I enclose: ☐ Check   ☐ Money order

Please send more information:

PARENT NAME: _____

ADDRESS: _____

TELEPHONE _____ E-MAIL _____

PARENT LIBRARY VOLUNTEER ORIENTATION
Volunteer Letter

GREAT EXPECTATIONS: Library Volunteer Staff
The success of the school library media program depends on the quality and productivity of the personnel responsible for the program. Volunteers can give valuable assistance and serve as a link to the community to support the library's efforts.

As a member of the volunteer staff, you can expect personal help, "inside" privileges, and an individualized program to match your interests and skills, as well as chances to

- Learn more about the school and the library: information, reading, research, technology,
- Do a variety of activities or to specialize,
- Explore the library science profession,
- Work with like-minded volunteers and adults,
- Make a difference, and
- Have fun—and occasionally food!

Typical library activities:
- Circulation, main desk coverage
- Storytelling and reading aloud
- Tutoring and research assistance
- Word processing and design
- Technical assistance
- Book and magazine processing
- Filing and shelving
- Videotaping
- Display and artwork
- Reviewing and writing

Librarian expectations of you, the volunteer staff:
- Dependability
- On-task behavior
- Willingness
- Courtesy and respect to all library users and staff
- Ability to learn the job and ask for help when you need it
- Self-direction when a skill is mastered

In turn, you may expect the library staff to
- Be courteous and respectful
- Train and support you so you can do your job
- Give you opportunities for growth

Process:
- Match interests and needs
- Learn the skill
- Perform it independently
- Acquire more skills

SKILLS CHECKLIST: Here is a checklist of skills used in performing duties in the library. Mark those skills you already have, those you would like to learn, and those you want to avoid. The skills are then matched with the specific library task.

- ☐ Filing
- ☐ Answering telephones
- ☐ Typing
- ☐ Word processing
- ☐ Organizing
- ☐ Writing
- ☐ Reviewing

- ☐ Illustrating
- ☐ Lettering
- ☐ Videotaping
- ☐ Photographing
- ☐ Mechanical work (carpentry, machine maintenance, lifting)
- ☐ Fine motor skills (folding, stamping)
- ☐ Cleaning
- ☐ Researching
- ☐ Tutoring
- ☐ Public speaking
- ☐ Reading aloud
- ☐ Storytelling
- ☐ Computer installing
- ☐ Computer programming

As the librarian interviews you about your present skills and goals, you may negotiate with the librarian for the best placement.

DISTRICT VOLUNTEER POLICIES AND PROCEDURES:

Volunteering in this district can be a satisfying way to contribute to the education of the community's children. In order to effectively utilize the time and talents of school volunteers, the district maintains volunteer personnel policies.

Applications and references: All volunteers must complete a volunteer application form. All volunteers working directly with students or working with information about students must also submit two personal references. All volunteers must also complete a form attesting to the fact that they have read, understood, and agreed to follow district policies. Completed forms are maintained by the district and school volunteer coordinator. All information provided in the application process is treated confidentially, but the district may use any application or reference information for documentation purposes when refusing to allow a volunteer to work in, or releasing a volunteer from, a position involving direct contact with students or fiscal responsibility.

JOB DESCRIPTION FOR VOLUNTEER LIBRARY AIDE

FUNCTIONS OF LIBRARY AIDES:
- To help maintain the library in efficient working order.
- To acquire specialized skills and knowledge of various library procedures.

Duties: Most library aides will be assigned one or more of the following tasks:
- Working at the charge or circulation desk
- Shelving books
- Reading shelves
- Updating and filing magazines
- Creating displays and bulletin boards
- Assisting with special projects

PROCEDURES:
- All library aides are to report as scheduled.
- Assignments will be given at the time of reporting.
- General school policies and rules are to be followed in the library.
- Library aides are expected to be courteous and helpful to others at all times.

I have read and understand this job description and agree to accept the privileges and responsibilities described in it. I also understand that if I do not perform satisfactorily, I give up the privilege of working in the library.

_____   _____
Volunteer's signature   Date

All volunteers are selected on the basis of understanding and accepting district and school policies and missions and willingness to comply with the application and referencing process, to perform the job, to participate in orientation and training, and to adhere to safety standards as set forth by the district and school.

Volunteer development: Volunteers have the opportunity to receive training in order to perform their functions competently. Each volunteer is evaluated regularly in writing by his immediate supervisor. Evaluation is based on performance and adherence to district and site policies. Discussion also includes the volunteer's satisfaction with the job and individual career needs. The school volunteer coordinator keeps copies of the evaluation.

Health and safety: Student health and safety are the district's and school's prime consideration. As responsible adults, volunteers should model positive role behaviors. District policy regarding the use and possession of drugs and alcohol is that no volunteer may use, possess, transfer, distribute, manufacture, or sell alcohol or any illegal drug while on school or district property, while on duty, or while operating a vehicle or potentially dangerous equipment that is owned or leased by the district or school. No volunteer may work for the school while under the influence of or impaired by any illegal drug or alcohol.

Sexual harassment is defined as unwelcome sexual advances, request for sexual favors and other verbal or physical conduct of a sexual nature that creates an intimidating, hostile, or offensive environment. It is illegal and against policies for any volunteer to sexually harass another volunteer, school employee, or student.

Resignation: A volunteer may terminate services prior to the end of the term of appointment by giving written notice to the immediate supervisor and school volunteer coordinator as far in advance as possible.

Sometimes a person is placed in a volunteer position for which he is not best suited, his behavior is not compatible with the mission and policies of the school, or he does not fulfill the description of the volunteer position. It may be necessary to encourage the person to resign or for the school to terminate that person. The district can terminate a person with or without cause at any time. Involuntary termination should always involve the school volunteer coordinator. Encouraged resignation and termination should be done only after careful consideration of the situation and person involved. The personnel involved should

- Maintain confidentiality, whenever possible,
- Consider evaluation and assessment, and
- Discuss the situation with the volunteer to determine facts.

The district recognizes the importance of providing a prompt and efficient procedure for resolution of a grievance. A complaint is defined as an allegation that conflict has occurred in the interpretation of school policy, practice, or procedure. Most volunteers who have a grievance or a conflict are encouraged to follow these procedures:

- Discuss informally with the school volunteer coordinator.
- If the issue has not been resolved, the second step is a discussion with the principal.
- If resolution of the grievance or conflict has not occurred, the volunteer should then discuss the grievance with the volunteer coordinator.

Site acknowledgment: I acknowledge that I have received and read the volunteer personnel policies on volunteer application and selection, development, health and safety, and resignation. I understand that the violation of any of these policies may result in the termination of my volunteer services for the affiliated school district.

PLEASE PRINT NAME: _____

ADDRESS: _____

SCHOOL: _____

SIGNATURE AND DATE: _____

I. ORIENTATION. The first encounter with the library staff member is the most important, for it establishes the relationship between the two persons. Moreover, it also paves the way for effective library use of volunteers.

The first encounter should include the basics: the library's mission, an overview of library functions, the role of library volunteer staff, the role of the other staff and their relationship to students, and the specific contributions and goals of the individual volunteer. The librarian needs to set forth the basic expectations of the volunteer and the volunteer's expectations of the library staff. The librarian should use the volunteer's application as the foundation for the interview and build upon the volunteer's strengths.

By the time the interview is finished, the volunteer should have some idea of direction, a sense of the librarian, and a feeling of anticipation for starting as a staff member. The librarian should have an idea of the volunteer's capabilities and interests, time commitment, and way of interacting with others.

In some cases, the librarian may end the interview by drawing up a written contract between the library and volunteer that will lay a concrete foundation for future relationships and provide a model for future work experiences. In any case, expectations should be clarified from the start. If the volunteer does not agree with the expectations, then he will probably not be comfortable helping in the library. It is much easier for the volunteer to opt out of the program at the beginning and not lose face or time than to get involved with a program that is unsuitable and difficult to leave later.

An orientation to the library, describing its services, is essential, for it makes it easier for volunteers to see the working environment and their place in the total picture. This tour also gives the rest of the staff an opportunity to meet the volunteer. Typically, the librarian tours the facility with the volunteer and describes the tasks associated with each part of the library:

- Circulation desk: student check-out/in, generative overdue notices
- Magazine rack: checking in magazines and filing them
- Display area: creating attractive displays and signs
- Pamphlet file: clipping and filing articles
- Computer stations: installing, inputting, troubleshooting, instructing, word processing, graphics
- Workroom: processing, repairing, withdrawing, producing

At that time, safety and emergency issues should also be discussed.

Orientation Learning Objectives:
By the end of the session the volunteers will be able to
- Describe the role of the volunteer within the library setting,
- Explain library policy and procedures regarding volunteer work,
- Identify basic library operations,
- Define basic library terms,
- Describe staff and student relationships, and
- List at least five skills to help students become independent learners.

Training resources:
- Library volunteer guide
- Flip chart, newsprint or chalkboard
- Pencils, pens, coloring tools
- Handouts on library terms and DDC
- Optional: overhead projector, VCR

> An orientation to the library, describing its services, is essential, for it makes it easier for volunteers to see the working environment and their place in the total picture.

Trainer notes:
- Use this experiential learning cycle: experience > share > process > generalize > apply. Always process.
- For large group reporting out, ask for sample responses.
- Consider having an assistant to act as a recorder and gofer.
- Don't force anyone to participate.
- Provide "stretch" break.

II. BASIC OPERATIONS. All volunteer staff should know how to perform basic library operations: circulation, filing and shelving, notices, and inventory. These services are ongoing and necessary for the smooth working of the library. Volunteers should feel comfortable filling in when any of these tasks need to be done. For instance, if book carts are piling up, volunteer staff should take it upon themselves to get those sources onto the shelves so students can use them.

In fact, this spirit of helpful service needs to be emphasized before anything else. Since volunteer staff represent the library, they need to know basic library protocols such as desk transactions and general interactions with library users and staff.

Next, volunteers need to be familiar with library jargon since it is used by staff and needs to be understood by library users. Trained volunteer staff can act as translators for students when, for example, the librarian casually tells a student to look for the call number and the volunteer staff member sees a blank look on the student's face.

Since a basic library service is the circulation of its resources, volunteer staff should know how to make that happen. Part of that function is to treat the borrower in a friendly and courteous manner; presentation is as important as function. Volunteer staff also need to learn how to field questions, since most of the school considers anyone behind the desk to be a library expert. An amazing number of questions are locational or basic: "Where is the pencil sharpener?" and "How can I find a fiction book?" Volunteer staff can field such inquiries, freeing the reference librarian to contend with sophisticated reference questions.

Students can use those resources that they can locate: in catalogs, in files, and on the shelves. Thus, a prime job of volunteer staff is to file and shelve. While some knowledge of the Dewey Decimal Classification system is useful because it gives volunteers a rationale for the arrangement of materials, attention to detail is actually more important, because an out-of-sequence source or entry is essentially a lost item.

> In fact, this spirit of helpful service needs to be emphasized before anything else.

Because materials need to be in constant circulation to maximize their use, timely overdue notices constitute a valuable service to the student body and faculty. Volunteer staff assist in this process by making sure that information is correct and notices are efficiently distributed.

Finally, the library needs to know what materials it truly has on hand. Nothing is more frustrating and misleading to users than to look at a library catalog and think that a specific resource is available, only to find a gap where the book or magazine should be. The librarian needs an accurate inventory to have an accurate picture of library holdings. While it is disheartening to discover missing or lost volumes, it is worse not to know about those gaps. At least with knowledge, the librarian can replace those important volumes. The volunteer staff's responsibility is to accurately report the status of every resource.

III. GUIDELINES TO LIBRARY VOLUNTEER EVALUATION.
Volunteers bring strength to the educational program. To more effectively utilize their time and talents, a volunteer coordinating system is in place, an essential part of which is an annual performance evaluation.

Job performance evaluation, and supervision in general, reinforce and recognize positive performance, promote growth and self-development, and change or modify negative or ineffective behavior. Conducting performance reviews involves a partnership between volunteer and supervisor, whether that supervisor is a paid staff member or another volunteer. These guidelines help establish and maintain that partnership:

Accepting a volunteer assignment: The job description for each volunteer position in the educational program forms the basis for the specific responsibilities the volunteer will be assuming and serves as the basis for the performance evaluation. Each volunteer will receive a copy of that job description when he is placed in a position. When a volunteer accepts a position, the supervisor and the volunteer will come to an agreement on the priority to be attached to each responsibility in the job description.

Evaluation of the volunteer job performance: A performance review will be completed at the end of the term of the volunteer assignment. Before the performance review, both supervisor and volunteer should review the job description and the agreed-upon priorities and rate the level of volunteer performance on those responsibilities.

The volunteer and supervisor should meet face-to-face to review and discuss the ratings. Both ratings should be recorded on a single form, which should then be signed by both parties.

At the conclusion of the evaluation meeting, they should identify potential areas of skill development for the volunteer and ways to achieve them, including new responsibilities and training.

▶ COMMUNITY

School libraries are local institutions and, as such, should interact closely with their publics. Increasingly, students learn in the community, and the community helps direct education. Librarians can help build powerful coalitions to accomplish mutual goals by

- Building on existing systems such as local chambers of commerce or community coalitions,
- Developing hotlines and community databases of information and experts,
- Enlisting the help of youth in local organizations,
- Attending, speaking to, and serving on committees of local groups,
- Training community members,
- Seeking partnerships with local groups,
- Hosting events for community groups, and
- Providing background research for community members.

Businesses are a "hot" source of partnerships today. Increasingly, they work with schools to offer assistance and school-to-career opportunities. Even educational grants look for evidence of business partnerships in support of school efforts. Some specific actions involving libraries include

- Providing and repairing library computers,
- Having library aides videotape business practices for a career exploration collection,
- Having library aides design Web sites for nonprofit organizations,
- Providing computer space on business servers for library Web pages, and
- Providing PR advice and forums for publicity relative to library campaigns.

One community institution is particularly important for library partnerships: local colleges and universities. Not only do their libraries need to articulate with K-12 educators, but programs that prepare teachers offer a wonderful opportunity for librarians to plant the seed for future educational partnerships. Just as entering administrators should have certain information literacy skills, so too should entering classroom teachers. Librarians can team-teach with college instructors to model curricular planning. School libraries can become a home base for student teachers and a testing area for technology skills. Librarians should seek out student teachers, providing them with insights gleaned from experience—and learning from entering professionals about current teaching theory that can be transformed into improved student achievement.

The Apple Library of Tomorrow grant program exemplifies community partnerships with libraries. The following grant combines high school and postsecondary collaboration with a business opportunity:

> ...programs that prepare teachers offer a wonderful opportunity for librarians to plant the seed for future educational partnerships.

Apple Partners in Education Grant Proposal

ABSTRACT. Redwood High School will work with Dominican College to provide pre- and inservice multimedia telecommunications teacher training on school-to-work (STW) skills that students can transfer to communications fields. Using an interdisciplinary approach, librarians and teachers in applied technology, art, and English will incorporate STW technology-aided projects so that students can actively pursue their own career interests. Community professionals in communication will also work with teachers, librarians, and students on these projects, so that students can experience real-life successful STW transitions. This focus will serve as a pilot test to be expanded throughout the school's curriculum.

GOALS AND BENEFITS OF PARTNERSHIP. The partnership offers a chance for pre- and inservice teachers to become competent in multimedia skills and teaching strategies, particularly as they apply to school-to-work transitions in the area of communication and enable the college to test new ways of training teachers and incorporating school-to-work with a representative high school student body.

Both institutions promote professional teacher development. Not only does Dominican College provide a wide range of preservice training, but it also has an active continuing education program in which Redwood faculty have acted as instructors. Redwood has adopted a new, thorough professional development program that fosters lifelong learning and classroom implementation of new skills. Dominican College brings its growing educational technology training program expertise with increased incorporation of technology into fine and language arts. Redwood offers a fertile ground for teacher-training pilot-testing: a chance for research and practice to merge.

This year, a school-to-work (STW) initiative was introduced to Redwood. A district STW coordinator works with the Marin County Office of Education (MCOE) and Redwood committees to formulate effective strategies. The high school art department offers a photography course combining esthetics and technical skills which complements a newly created multimedia option in a computer applications course. This project also fits into the English department's desire to offer more courses in communications, especially in the publication field. The library offers access to technology throughout the day.

This project will serve as action research to discover what practices make a significant difference in student achievement and preparation for STW transitions. The project will also test a model of interdepartmental collaboration in teaching technical skills and practice. Dominican College, for its part, will research effective models for teaching STW concepts within the existing teacher training curriculum. It will also research the effectiveness of multimedia techniques in teacher training.

This project provides the equipment for practical-scale teacher training and schoolwork in a multimedia environment, which is presently not available. With the emphasis on school-to-work transitions and a focus on communications careers, this grant provides multimedia tools to reach these goals.

Providing equipment for classes and the library at both sites makes cross-curriculum and cross-institutional efforts feasible. Moreover, multimedia-enhanced instructional and assessment methods can be tested and transferred in a controlled environment, with a focus on STW communications skills.

TARGET POPULATION. The target population is three-fold: Dominican teacher candidates, Redwood High School teachers and Redwood High School students. The primary focus is students having an interest in communications (media, fine arts, journalism) or computers. This project also addresses the needs of limited-English and physically challenged students because of the visual aspects of multimedia. The overall targeting decision is based on WASC (Western Association of Schools and Colleges) and site council recommendations, which have highlighted the needs of a diverse student population and reinforcement of school-to-work preparation.

In terms of curriculum, this project involves several departments—fine arts, technical arts, and English—through a communications strand. Curriculum will address STW and articulation with higher education institutions; students will be able to explore career options such as graphic communications, photojournalism, architecture, publishing, and training. The project will also involve local communications professionals who will come to the sites to reinforce STW articulation.

Student interests factor heavily in curriculum development. Within courses, students can determine which projects to pursue based on their interests. Faculty can use student surveys and focus groups to develop courses. The curriculum will take into account student participation in clubs such as photography and video. This project works best in an interdisciplinary context. Technical arts can provide the technical skills, photography will teach both technical skills and application options, and English will provide additional application opportunities. For some existing electives, students may receive credit in one or two disciplines. The STW committee will work with these departments to further heighten interdisciplinary efforts.

Of particular note is the Senior Projects option; students design their own course as a means of nontraditional learning in an area of their choice, irrespective of school disciplines. The project will give students the chance to explore communications career avenues of personal interest.

With Apple computer technology, teachers can present coursework in a more interactive way, and students can share their research findings in exciting multimedia format as they learn STW skills. For example, in an arts exploratory course, students can scan images of a famous artist and modify his or her works using illustration computer programs in order to explore style and artistic concepts. In photography, they can scan and edit images for artistic and editorial presentations. CAD courses can design projected school renovations. Journalism students can produce multimedia news programs. Student products can be broadcast so the community at large can be inspired to create their own projects.

During the second year, program opportunities can be expanded because of increased access to equipment, particularly in the library. Additionally, students and teachers who will have been trained in multimedia techniques can teach others in different disciplines so a broader base of students can learn those technical skills and apply them to their own STW interests.

DIRECTIONS FOR THE TEACHER TRAINING INSTITUTION. Both Dominican student teachers and practicing Redwood teachers are slated to participate in the program. The core of the project will comprise teacher candidates at Redwood and teachers in technical arts, fine arts, English, and the library. This broad-based STW communications focus takes advantage of Dominican's strong humanities and arts program and should help strengthen Redwood's offerings. Through this program, pre- and inservice teachers should become more proficient in combining STW preparation with communication and technology; moreover, they should develop more interactive instruction that meets the varied learning needs of a diverse student population.

Specific competencies and outcomes will include practice and research about increased incorporation of school-to-work issues in teacher training with transference to teacher practice and innovative uses of multimedia technology for pre- and inservice training, particularly teaching STW communications skills with transference to teacher practice. On the college level, seminars and continuing education courses are customized to meet student and teacher needs. At the unit level, multimedia instruction can address adolescent STW needs and interests and so motivate teachers to become involved and succeed.

In teacher training, Apple technology draws together the different types of resources available to teach students. Teacher trainers can videotape teacher candidate sessions and career sites to develop interactive programs that teach classroom and communication skills and bring the work world to the classroom. Teacher candidates can take photos of classroom and work practices, scan them, and create a multimedia montage about student diversity or work place options. Practicing teachers can develop multimedia presentations on STW concepts that teacher candidates can use in their coursework to develop a repertoire of teaching strategies.

DIRECTIONS FOR A K-12 SCHOOL AND TEACHER TRAINING INSTITUTION. Student-centered learning is emphasized in both pre- and inservice training, since multimedia projects are the result of both student and teacher learning. Teachers and students work collaboratively as they explore the media's capabilities. Students bring their interests and openness; teachers bring experience and subject expertise. The communications emphasis is a natural for student-centered learning because students use multimedia to create their own projects. School-to-work transitions also allow students to explore individual career paths. Some specific strategies include

- Having students photograph and videotape work places for student multimedia presentations,
- Inviting professionals from communications fields to teach students skills that incorporate technology,
- Videotaping student interviews and developing a multimedia training kit for student use, and
- Having students develop multimedia portfolios to use in job interviews.

To develop these projects, students will use both Apple-supplied and school-provided software. *ClarisWorks* and MS *Office* offer sophisticated tools for written and statistical expression. *HyperStudio* and MS *PowerPoint* allow the user to coordinate graphics and text creatively. Redwood and Dominican College have other media applications to enrich student products: *Ofoto, Hyperscan, Photoshop*, Apple *Media Kit, SuperPaint, Illustrator, Premiere,* and *Director.* Other software may be purchased if it demonstrates an ability to be incorporated into multimedia products with particular emphasis on STW or communications techniques (and has excellent reviews).

The two sites work within the same community: southern Marin. Redwood has a Business-Education Roundtable to provide local technical expertise in communications work. Redwood's Two-Plus-Two program, which links high school work with junior college courses, can be incorporated into the project. Dominican College provides a forum for professional communicators and technicians to share their insights; they can work with staff to develop lessons that incorporate multimedia into career exploration.

In order to evaluate whether the project is effective, Dominican College will design the following assessments to be used by both sites for baseline and formative evaluation:
- Student and teacher surveys of course satisfaction,
- Sample reviews of student and teacher projects and portfolios by the core team,
- Course registration statistics,
- Student and teacher candidate grades, and
- Observation of classroom activity by the core team.

WHAT THE PROJECT WILL LOOK LIKE. At the third month, a visitor would see designs for workshops on using multimedia technology to incorporate STW and communications skills. Teacher-trainers and teacher candidates would jointly produce multimedia presentations for classrooms. Some high school students would be learning alongside teachers, pilot-testing instructional strategies that related to STW and communications skills.

At the sixth month, a visitor would see teachers and teacher candidates incorporating their new skills in the classroom. Teachers and students would synthesize their learning experience into multimedia products. Students in technical arts, photography, and journalism would present communications projects through multimedia. Seniors would design semester projects promoting career exploration in communications fields. Dominican faculty would begin to test the effectiveness of their multimedia pre- and inservice training.

At the end of one year, teachers (both pre- and inservice) would use multimedia presentations to teach their students units to fit youngsters' interests. They would also begin to train other teachers to enhance instructional and learning strategies for STW transitions. Students would produce more multimedia reports, and libraries would archive them. Students would work with teachers to help design course delivery. More sources would incorporate STW skills training through multimedia technology experiences, and team teaching both within and between institutions would be encouraged and practiced. A wide spectrum of students would feel empowered through expertise, control of learning, and readiness for life beyond high school.

▸ PROFESSIONAL PEERS

Particularly since many school libraries have only one professional library teacher, collaboration with peers is necessary to maintain high quality service. Public and other types of libraries can offer substantial support.

A beginning step is to exchange information about collections and services.

- Which of these would be available to each other—and each other's constituents?
- Are there projects that could be done more effectively together, such as summer reading programs or internships?
- How might resource sharing be improved through partnerships?
- Could grants be co-sponsored?
- Could professional development be coordinated?

The more often librarians of all sorts talk with each other, the more they can support and advocate each other.

Another way to foster librarian partnerships is to work in each other's environment. School librarians sometimes substitute in public libraries during the summer while regular staff vacation. The public librarian might booktalk at the school or participate on the school's library council. Librarians can help each other support student classwork and find ways to acquire needed resources. If the public librarian sees students struggling with a particular information literacy skill, such as evaluating Web sites, he can alert his school counterpart that more instruction in that area is needed. Particularly if either librarian has a school-age child, their interactions may become routine.

Partnerships can also assume a formal nature in local or regional professional organizations. Librarian groups can develop projects and get state or national funding to support those efforts. Some examples include developing periodical union catalogs,

✓ CHECKLIST FOR PARTNERSHIPS WITH LOCAL LIBRARIES

☐ Do you have a list of local school, public, government, and special libraries?

☐ Do you know their librarians?

☐ Do you communicate regularly with local school and public libraries?

☐ Do you let public libraries know about major research assignments?

☐ Do you exchange holdings lists of periodicals, indexes, special collections, or non-print items?

☐ Do you create union lists of these resources?

☐ Do you exchange booklists or instructional aids, either librarian- or teacher-generated?

☐ Do you help each other with collection development through reviewing, exchanging, donations, group purchasing, or collection specialization?

☐ Do you publicize each other's activities?

☐ Do you do joint programming: sharing speakers, displays, equipment?

☐ Do you tell students about opportunities at other libraries, either for work or recreation?

☐ Do you share professional materials or conference insights?

☐ Do you train one another or encourage group professional development?

☐ Do you support one another in library issues, such as school campaigns or library bonds?

(From *Leadership within the School Library and Beyond*, p. 8.2)

creating local agency hotline databases, establishing disaster planning and preservation centers, and coordinating facsimile article ILL delivery. Usually one library system acts as the fiscal agent, and the other libraries sign joint partner agreements to deal with governance issues. Obviously, such substantial projects require long-term commitment by both the librarians and their governing boards. The investment over time can really pay off, though.

The following questions help librarians who work in different settings support each other:

Library-related institutions and organizations can collaborate at the state level as well as the local one. Grants, in particular, benefit both levels: State departments provide funds for supporting exemplary practices, and local school libraries provide sites for pilot-testing educational innovations. The dissemination of information about successful projects enables other libraries throughout the state and nation to implement these new ideas on a broad scale.

Here is one such grant application that shows how educational agencies can work together to help students:

Library Services and Technology Act (LSTA) Grant Proposal

PROJECT TITLE: Information Resources for Students with Special Needs

JURISDICTION: Marin County

PROJECT SUMMARY: This project is intended to provide information resources and services for students with special needs through school librarians developing and managing a shared collection of software and hardware to serve middle and high school students in Marin County public schools. The project is a demonstration model, since this kind of coordinated service, incorporating adaptive technology, is a vanguard effort.

This project was inspired by talks with special education (SE) and mainstream teachers as well as observations and discussions by school librarians. In surveying the county population's needs, the teachers and the technical specialist inventoried available resources for special education students and noted the lack of adaptive technology for them and the success that such students have had with technology and related resources. For example, Redwood High School library now offers audiocassette books that help students with special needs "read" their required novels.

Students with special needs have difficulty accessing information because of vision disabilities (can't read small text; may be blind), limited movement (can't type or sit at workstation) and comprehension problems (can't understand mainstream resources). Presently, these students use school libraries to a limited extent; they are accompanied by an aide who does much of the access work. Because of budget limitations, neither school libraries nor special education classrooms can afford much adaptive technology. Instead, the funds, most of which are categorical, go to pay salaries for this labor-intensive program. In short, this group of students is underserved.

Latest figures put this population at over 10 percent of the total student population. Over the past five years, the conscious effort to serve them under new legislative measures has impacted all staff, special and regular. Even though Marin County is considered a well-to-do area, some of its students experience great frustration because they need accommodations to receive an equitable education. Students are increasingly mainstreamed but do not have the resources to participate equitably. Particularly with the passage of the Americans with Disabilities Act, schools have a greater responsibility than ever to serve these young people.

Now aware of the situation and the possibility of funding, middle and high school librarians in Marin public schools, through their Marin School Librarians group, planned how to offer services for these students. They attended library conferences that dealt with this issue and researched existing programs. At present, the two main California programs are run out of Los Angeles and Sacramento; neither focuses on K-12 students, and the latter's delivery service is unrealistically slow for students. Locally, a few academic libraries have acquired adaptive technologies. However, other states do not appear to have inter-school-related library services.

Since they would be breaking ground on an important service, the school librarians talked with their special education teachers as well as the county coordinators who administer this program. Together, they inventoried available resources and drew up a list of needed adaptive technology and resources. For example, *Ultimate Reader*, a new advanced literacy development system, adds spoken voice and visual highlighting to print or electronic text. The Marin Company Synapse has worked with academic libraries to provide such technologies. In addition to these access tools, print and nonprint (video, CD-ROM, audio) materials are being selected that will be relevant to these and other students.

The librarians designed a means to organize and distribute the technology so it could be housed throughout the Special Education Local Planning Area (SELPA) and circulated upon need. In that way, a few pieces of equipment will be available to all, so students would indeed have local access to the material they need when they request it. The plan also includes training in technology use and incorporation, the audience being special education and mainstream teachers as well as school librarians. The training is also being co-designed by special education teachers and school librarians with help from Synapse, Dominican College, and Sonoma State University.

PLAN OUTLINE WITH TARGET DATES: Special education teachers and librarians will
- Assess present resources for special education students (1-8/98),
- Select and acquire appropriate resources (8-9/98),
- Organize and distribute resources (librarians only—(11-12/98),
- Train educators on use of resources (1/99-3/99), and
- Evaluate student and educator success (1-4/99).

A steering committee, with representation from each of the stakeholder groups, will coordinate the effort. They will also consult with Dominican College's special education program and Sonoma State University's services for students with special needs. Since the special education program extends to 18-22-year-olds, this pilot program's resources and services will be available to the college's and university's special needs students as well as those at the College of Marin. The targeted students will be expected to improve their literacy and class participation rate, which will be assessed through authentic performance, IEP review, reference-based tests, and observation. Educators will exhibit increased use of adaptive strategies to involve students. Librarians will maintain circulation, planning, and training records to demonstrate increased service.

Because the grant is for capital purchases and training, its benefits will far outlast its funding period. The money provides the basis for resources and their use. Once a threshold number of materials are available and basic training is conducted, additional items can be purchased more readily, and service can expand. The intent is that the successful implementation of this demonstration program will convince both district and county funding sources to support continued and expanded services.

Personnel costs will be used for training design and implementation. A train-the-trainer model will be used to maximize benefits. A core of librarians, special education teachers, and mainstream teachers will receive the first training. They will, in turn, train their peers.

Middle and high school libraries throughout SELPA will share library materials and related adaptive technology equipment. Thus, each site will not have to purchase all of its own equipment, possibly duplicating efforts elsewhere. Instead, they can be assured a basic set of needed materials and can rotate the more sophisticated technology as needed. Representative materials will include science and cultural videotapes, audiobooks, reference CD-ROMs, art books, vocational guidance sources, and math software. Representative adaptive technologies will include scanning equipment, voice-activated software, adaptive keyboards, interactive tablets, and enlargement equipment.

Probably the greatest benefit of this project is the collaboration among Marin County school librarians, special education teachers, and mainstream teachers. Resources will be available more equitably and quickly as technology is effectively incorporated into the library and classroom. This model program can be replicated elsewhere to provide needed information and service to people with special needs.

How Do Partnerships Grow?

*Teamwork: coming together is beginning;
keeping together is progress; working together is success.
A partnership is like a living organism and needs careful tending
and nurturing—and occasional pruning.*

▶ GROUNDWORK

As with most healthy plants, the better the bedding, the better the bloom. What is the condition of the school's "soil"? Is the school's culture so sandy that partnerships don't "stick"? Or are expectations so muddy that good intentions sink? Maybe school practices are choked with weeds. Do rocks of contention need to be removed? Fortunately, most education grounding can be improved. Sometimes baked-in mindsets need to be broken up or churned to introduce air. Other times outside ideas can fertilize school thinking. In other cases, watering a parched culture can do the job.

However, to paraphrase Voltaire, librarians need to tend their own gardens first. Collection development, facilities management, and human resource supervision should meet and exceed standards. Librarians need to make sure their own crop is flourishing before they start plowing other fields. Besides, when others see prize-winning results in the library, they'll want to take time to smell those roses—and pick some for themselves.

Regardless of the situation, librarians must pay attention to the school's environment and do the necessary digging around to optimize the planting of partnerships. Continuing the metaphor, one can approach gardening in several ways. A corner plot may look ready for a new bed of posies. Or one may purchase a tray of budding plants and then look for a spot to plant them. These activities correspond to using the school's informal system: attracting individuals or meeting groups and planning and implementing one-time activities with a few people. On the other hand, gardening can be done systematically. In developing partnerships, this translates into using existing system structures or creating them: joining committees and establishing library boards or steering committees. It should be noted that such formal work usually requires administrative support since the librarian is, metaphorically, in the community's garden patch.

▶ THE GARDEN SHOWS

The hardest part of partnering can sometimes be starting the relationship. Moving from the comfort zone to the unknown can be scary. Beginning friendships recall that same kind of hopeful nervousness. In the most natural situation, two people are attracted to each other, seeing qualities and values in each other that resonate with them.

Of course, for friendships or partnerships to happen, there has to be a level of awareness. Think of the number of movies that play upon that theme: missed opportunities because one person didn't notice another until that special moment. A state of constant awareness may well serve as a starting point for growing partnerships. Particularly for librarians who are not used to pro-active outreach, maintaining a good library and looking for opportunities to respond sensitively to others' interests can be a comfortable way to start relationships. Some tips for such an approach follow:

Genuine caring and attractiveness give the library a friendly atmosphere.

- Does the school community feel welcome in the library?
- Does a spirit of active learning exist there?
- Is there a spot for teachers to work or to relax?
- Is there a sense of order and calm that invites others to explore?

For many, the library is a safe haven in a chaotic world, a stimulating home base where students and staff can take intellectual and creative risks without threat.

Beyond an attractive atmosphere, the library must offer a clear menu of resources and services. Library brochures listing collection numbers, square footage, and staff aren't very interactive. Rather, the library should be described in terms of the users' active needs: exploring careers, making transparencies for the classroom, getting sample driver's tests, finding diagrams to aid in a dissection project, or holing up in a quiet corner to read a mystery. The more specific examples cited, the more real the library becomes.

One clever way to make others aware of the library is to develop a survey. (Oh, no, not another survey!) Simply asking community members how often they use the library for different purposes subtly communicates what the library has to offer; it's a quick educational tool. Of course, the survey should be short and professional; that initial image is as important on paper as it is in person. To build the image of the library as a high-tech center, librarians can put the survey online on their Web pages. In any case, the survey results let the librarian know which areas need to be emphasized. That valuable input helps establish direction for building partnerships—which seeds to plant where.

The librarian tries to match needs to library resources, which requires active observation and listening. Needs may be curriculum-based or personal, intellectual or social. A teacher may need to develop a summer reading list: *voila*—the librarian's suggestions! A parent may need a good novel for escape: *voici*—the bestseller or golden oldie! What to do with students who whiz through the material? Have them create hyper-

> For many, the library is a safe haven in a chaotic world, a stimulating home base where students and staff can take intellectual and creative risks without threat.

media stacks in the library as tutorials for slower achievers.

Especially as librarians work with the school community over time, they see the difference between needs and wants. Teachers may *want* the librarian to hand-pick useful Web sites for students, but what teachers may *need* is help in instructing students in methods of evaluating online resources. Students may *want* more days in the library to conduct research when what they may actually *need* are more ways to research more effectively and use their time more wisely. The trickiest point is the means to address those wants *and* needs gracefully and respectfully. Librarians, too, may express their own wants more than their needs. The savvy teacher may offer valuable insights that will help librarians gain entry into teachers' lounges and curriculum development teams. Students who are given individual attention can pass on positive word to their peers. Well-grounded partnerships are the key to the honest communication required to negotiate sensitive issues of wants and needs.

Here is one such survey, which can be used to educate staff:

MAKE THE LIBRARY CONNECTION

By completing this survey of your library use, you will help us improve library services for you and your students.

1. How often do your assignments require student use of the library?
   ☐ Weekly   ☐ Monthly   ☐ Quarterly   ☐ Each semester

2. Which of the following assignments requiring library time do you give? (Check all that apply.)
   ☐ Research reports ☐ Oral reports   ☐ Debates   ☐ Book reports
   ☐ Current events   ☐ Biographies   ☐ Fiction   ☐ Specific facts
   ☐ Pictures   ☐ Computer use   ☐ Internet   ☐ Other:

3. What services of the library do you use? (Check all that apply.)
   ☐ Instruction on accessing sources   ☐ Instruction on evaluating sources
   ☐ Assistance as needed by students   ☐ Develop or provide book lists, guides
   ☐ Pre-selecting sources   ☐ Bookmarking Web sites
   ☐ Planning   ☐ Other

4. The librarian is helpful in making suggestions about materials that might be useful to your students. (Please circle one.)
   Strongly agree   Agree   Disagree   Strongly disagree

5. The librarian is helpful in assisting your students with their library work when asked.
   Strongly agree   Agree   Disagree   Strongly disagree

6. The librarian has an adequate collection in your subject area.
   Strongly agree   Agree   Disagree   Strongly disagree

7. How would you rate the library as a help to you in teaching?
   Essential   Important   Useful   Not useful

8. The library is useful for your own research or pleasure reading.
   Strongly agree   Agree   Disagree   Strongly disagree

Please complete the following sentences:

9. I see the greatest strengths of our library program to be

10. I recommend that the library program also include

11. I'd just like to say: *(Please make any additional comments on the back of this sheet.)*

Thank you, again, for helping to make our library even better.

A scavenger hunt approach is an effective way to educate students about library services:

 LIBRARY SCAVENGER HUNT

DIRECTIONS: Different parts of the library are labeled with an alphabet letter. Write down the letter that corresponds to the numbered function (listed below) that you can do in the library.

1. Find the call number of a book
2. Find an atlas
3. Read a current magazine
4. Make a photocopy
5. Read a back issue of the school newspaper
6. Find a pamphlet on AIDS
7. Find a list of articles on a social issue
8. Word-process a report
9. Look up a word in a dictionary
10. Get background information from an encyclopedia
11. Use a CD-ROM magazine index
12. Locate a fiction book
13. Check out a book or magazine
14. Find a recent local newspaper
15. Find a two-month old newspaper
16. Read the computer rules
17. Look at displays
18. Use the online library catalog
19. Read current research on the Internet
20. Find a book list
21. Find out what books local libraries have
22. Scan a photo
23. Ask for help

▶ MEETING WITH GROUPS

Meeting wants and needs through developing partnerships requires getting out of the library, just as teachers can't use the library effectively behind their desks. Even when teachers have a computer in each classroom with access to the library's holdings, librarians need to meet with teachers on their own ground. In some cases, librarians may notice another person's "garden": high-quality efforts that could work well in the library's surroundings. For instance, the librarian may observe that a teacher works well with his or her students and assigns articulate, thought-provoking projects and thinks, "I'd like to work more closely with that person." Perhaps the librarian notices how well a particular student helps peers with computer problems and thinks that student would be a great library aide.

So while inviting groups into the library gives the librarian a chance to promote the library's program, librarians need to demonstrate that they mean business by meeting with groups professionally. What regular meetings occur? Do subject or grade level groups discuss issues on a consistent basis? What task forces need library input? By examining the school meeting schedule, librarians can encourage a broader perspective; they can actively participate in school affairs by attending these meetings.

While it is easier to just sit in on a meeting, it's usually a good idea to have a concrete reason for attending. It's a good opportunity to slant the library's resources and services to that group's specific needs. A librarian with a talent for mathematical recreational games can give a mini-lesson about Lewis Carroll's logic puzzles, getting the teachers involved, and follow the talk with a book list of math titles and an offer to give the presentation in their classes. When teachers see that librarians know about their subject areas, they may be more receptive to librarian partnerships.

By attending meetings, librarians hear about school problems:

- How can teachers help an increasingly diverse student population?
- What are different ways to assess student learning?
- How can students learn about current Latin American literary trends?
- How should the school approach the AIDS issue?

Librarians can offer their services by developing resource lists of in-house materials or local agencies. They can do research on the topic of concern. They can connect staff with experts in the field. They can work on ad hoc committees as equal partners in educational problem-solving. They can develop grant proposals to address issues.

All these efforts demonstrate to groups specific ways that librarians and libraries provide significant access to information—and ways to work with that information.

▶ PLANTING SEEDS

While partnerships can begin on a social basis, they can't be considered strong educationally unless substantive tasks are accomplished through them. To an extent, librarians can develop relationships based on insightful responsiveness, satisfying needs as they are identified. However, such an approach sets up a power imbalance where the librarian serves as a valuable handmaid-

> While it is easier to just sit in on a meeting, it's usually a good idea to have a concrete reason for attending. It's a good opportunity to slant the library's resources and services to that group's specific needs.

en or astute executive assistant. A subtle hierarchy is established that precludes an authentic partnership.

Thus, for powerful *partnerships* to develop, librarians must bring their own seeds to plant. How is that done? One seed at a time. As school community members experience the positive results of effective planning with librarians, they will seek opportunities to expand those partnerships. Essentially, librarians need to look at their own past experiences with the school community and think of ways to improve those conditions. Not only should they listen to others' concerns and ideas, responding effectively with feasible ideas for joint solutions, but librarians need to identify unspoken needs within the community and offer library-based solutions. The trick is to align library needs, such as information literacy skills, with other school concerns so joint problem-solving occurs, and each partner feels empowered.

Maybe a teacher wants students to have current information about biotechnology advances; a perfect opportunity for class instruction on information searching exists. The librarian and teacher can plan a period during which students can learn how to use periodical indexes, both in paper and CD-ROM, as well as Internet search engines, while gathering recent trends about biotechnology. The teacher can evaluate how well students tie in their findings to their classwork, and the librarian can evaluate how well students found and assessed information sources.

Perhaps students want to improve their rhetorical skills. The librarian can supply videotaping equipment and teach a crew how to tape, as well as work with the teacher on instructing students to critically view and evaluate speeches.

If in the past the librarian worked with students individually on Middle Ages assignments, pointing out to each one the many areas where information can be found, he might talk with the teacher and suggest that a "pathway" about the Middle Ages be produced, accompanied by a short presentation or scavenger hunt for relevant sources throughout the library. Perhaps the librarian can direct the teacher to an interactive WebQuest on the topic. If the resultant student work is more interesting and substantial than before, the teacher will be more open to partnering with the librarian in the future.

> The trick is to align library needs, such as information literacy skills, with other school concerns so joint problem-solving occurs, and each partner feels empowered.

SAMPLE PATHWAY GUIDE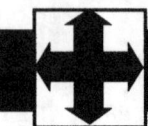

1. For general background information, use an encyclopedia [title of encyclopedia].
2. Generate a set of *keywords* or *terms* [suggest terms].
3. For specific facts, use *specialized reference books*, such as _____.
4. Some CD-ROM *reference titles* include _____.
5. For current information, consult *periodicals* by using a magazine index, such as _____.
6. Some specific periodicals in this field include _____.
7. For current information, also check the *Internet*. Remember to evaluate what you find because quality varies greatly. Some good sites include_____.
8. For in-depth information examine *books*. Use your keywords to locate books through the library's catalog. Some Dewey Decimal Classification call numbers in this field include_____.

PATHWAY TO ANCIENT GREECE AND ROME
Reference works:
- 103   Encyclopedia of philosophy
- 103   World philosophy
- 291.03 Mythology of all races
- 398.03 Dictionary of folklore
- 703   Praeger encyclopedia of art
- 503   McGraw-Hill encyclopedia of science and technology
- 609   History of technology
- 880.9 Ancient writers
- 902.09 Historical tables
- 909   Great events of history
- 91   historic atlases
- 920   McGraw-Hill encyclopedia of world biography
- 925   Concise dictionary of scientific biography
- 930   Concise encyclopedia of ancient civilization
- 937.03 Who was who in the Roman world
- 938   Oxford history of the classical world
- 938   Harper's dictionary of classical literature and antiquities

Web sites:

http://www.julen.net/ancient Ancient World Web meta-index

http://www.yahoo.com/Arts/Humanities/History/Ancient_History Ancient history links

http://www.hyperhistory.com Outline of history by date

Dewey Decimal numbers and their subjects:
- 190   Philosophy
- 291-2 Mythology
- 301.4 Women
- 305   Society: women, family, classes
- 355   War
- 370.9 Education
- 391   Costumes
- 394   Customs
- 473   Latin language
- 483   Greek language
- 509   History of science
- 510.9 History of math
- 520.9 History of astronomy
- 608   Inventions
- 610.9 History of medicine
- 623.4 Weapons
- 641.5 Food
- 709.37 Roman art
- 709.38 Greek art
- 780.9 History of music
- 790   Games and sports history
- 792   Theater history
- 870   Latin literature
- 880   Greek literature
- 909   World history
- 930   Ancient history
- 937   Roman history
- 938   Greek history

▶ PLOTTING PARTNERSHIPS

Once word gets around that the library has good resources and services, it's time to expand and formalize partnerships: to stake out an area to cultivate. The library needs official "blessing" as an active educational partner, particularly from administrators. Specific instructional and curricular roles need to be clarified so the entire school community understands the "garden varieties" of relationships. Still, educational partnerships with librarians should not be mandated from above, but rather be the natural result of schoolwide awareness and deliberation. If faculty don't own the decision, then it will be harder for the librarian to get cooperation.

A good way to develop this type of systemic backing, to define the partnership "bed," is to institute a library board or steering committee. Composed of teacher, administrative, parent and student representatives, this group can provide valuable insights into the workings of the school and the sometimes unvoiced needs that the library can address. These people act as ears for the librarian, outposts for those areas a librarian may not frequent. Perhaps students want leisure seating or magazines to cut up; perhaps teachers need a place to store papers or educational publications; perhaps administrators need workshops videotaped or a literature review on independent study programs.

Board members can also help solve library problems of theft, noise, and other library abuse by offering different solutions and enforcing subsequent library action. The group provides two-way communication and action between the school and the library—and can form the core of schoolwide library planning.

> A good way to develop this type of systemic backing, to define the partnership "bed," is to institute a library board or steering committee.

The advisory board also serve as library advocates, communicating library needs and services to the rest of the school. The group would be aware of a constrained library budget and could let others know of the library's dilemma, adding credence to librarian demands for more funds. The group could help determine and plan library events, ensuring wider participation before and during the program.

In one school, a science fiction conference was held in the library. Student techies demonstrated library CD-ROMs to the public, library interns made a maze for young attendees, the adults found a local science fiction writer who was honored at the event's reception, art teachers publicized a program cover contest, another teen group videotaped the day, and local merchants donated door prizes. As a result, 450 people came on a Saturday to enjoy a most successful event. This kind of participation would not have been possible without a well-established board acting as liaison and planners.

While some librarians align themselves with a specific department or other school subgroup, those who join schoolwide committees are probably in the best position politically. (In a few cases, librarians become part of the administrative team, but this managerial viewpoint is rare, unfortunately.) For long-term, significant partnerships, librarians should be permanent members of curriculum development committees. Not only do they get to see what courses and approaches are being considered, they also can help shape the curriculum and develop related courses. If librarians see valuable resources being overlooked, they can suggest course units that could take advantage of existing materials.

The more librarians can participate as active members of meaningful committees, the more they are regarded by others as substantial forces within the school—as equal partners in education. Librarians would be welcome additions to strategic planning and accreditation committees (two wonderful opportunities to understand school governance) as well as alternative instructional programs, such as contract work or independent study committees, inservice and professional development committees, and evaluation committees. Group members will value librarian resourcefulness, cross-discipline expertise, and helpfulness.

▶ MAKING THE GARDEN GROW

Once librarians are integrated into both the academic and informal systems in a school, they are in a position to offer a full range of library resources and services to the various constituencies. Together, they'll not only make the school system work for them, but help modify the system itself, thus making the school bloom.

Early on, a librarian might have to proceed cautiously, focusing effort on listening closely to the expressed needs of the school community. While that active listening must continue, eventually the librarian can become more active. Based on a strong mission statement constructed in partnership with the library board, the librarian can develop a range of objectives about resources and services, which can be prioritized depending on curriculum, staffing, finances, and student characteristics.

Since planning for growth is a given, the first list of services would be those that can be provided at present, using existing resources. A list might also include expanded offerings that need no additional material support. A farther-reaching list of services would include items that cannot be supplied now, but could benefit the school if more resources were available. The first list says, in effect, "Here are the library's resources for partnering now." The second list asserts, "Given sufficient resources and support, the library could *really* work with you by offering . . . ."

In developing a range of partnership opportunities, librarians can offer a menu from which the community can choose. In addition, as partnerships deepen, new ideas for collaboration arise. At that point, partners can prioritize their options.

A School Community-Developed Program

Information literacy. Students need to be able to locate, evaluate, interpret, organize, and share information. Both the process and the product must be addressed. This service is probably the core partnership activity. Some specifics include

- Articulate literacy skills instruction throughout the curriculum so concepts can be introduced and mastered in terms of subject areas.
- Create research units on using specialized reference sources so students can develop a repertoire of research strategies.
- Interview all students doing research papers, offering opportunities for the librarian to review student's strategies and suggest added sources to consider.
- Encourage peer instruction on using educational technology.
- Team-teach educators in information literacy using emerging technology.

Reading encouragement. The entire school community can work together to attract student readers by

> The second list asserts, "Given sufficient resources and support, the library could really work with you by offering . . . ."

- Creating bibliography bookmarks listing exciting books grouped by reading level or subject.
- Organizing book clubs, or give "Siskel and Ebert" reviews of new titles.
- Offering storytelling workshops so older students can read to eager younger ones.
- Giving holiday gift book ideas so parents can reinforce good reading habits at home.
- Starting a book chat room on the school's intranet as a forum for sharing good reading.
- Photographing the school community reading, creating custom "READ" posters.

Programs and events. Special events offer enrichment learning opportunities. Several approaches may be used:
- Co-sponsor author visits, either "live" or through videoconferencing.
- Conduct career and college nights for students and parents.
- Celebrate national library-related times such as Children's Book Week, Teen Read Week, Banned Books Week, Library Lovers Month.
- Co-produce curriculum-related events such as a Renaissance fair or a women's seminar.
- Team-teach parent workshops, such as Internet use or child development.

Collection development. A significant service of the library is to provide access to resources. Librarian-teacher partnerships can strengthen that objective by
- Expanding the professional collection.
- Working with ESL staff to include more multicultural resources, including photos and publications from foreign countries.
- Creating and annotating Web pages of useful research URLs.
- Building and weeding the collection collaboratively.

Archives. Libraries can also serve as repositories for original schoolwork:
- Student books and reports
- Student multimedia productions
- Teacher transparencies and slides collections
- Video documentaries about school life
- Student Web pages.

Displays. School community members can produce displays to provide dramatic, visual stimuli. These presentations may take the form of
- Exhibits of student projects, both artistic and textual
- Tie-ins with educational broadcasts
- Community exhibits and videos
- Curricular resources and student work based on those materials
- Realia with educational implications (a "gutted" computer, exotic instruments).

Products. The school community can produce library-related materials in various formats:
- Newsletters and Web pages to inform faculty and the larger community about library activities and needs
- Research and production guides
- Bibliographies to provide curricular support and advice for leisure readers
- Multimedia library orientations
- Binders of readings and research on technology or literacy
- Web pages of Net-based lesson ideas.

Fund-raising. As partners, librarians can support financial efforts on several fronts:
- Participate in each other's school fund-raisers to show school support.
- Foster adopt-a-book or computer program.
- Co-produce an educational technology fair.
- Sell customized stationery or produce

community Web sites using library technology.
- Locate grant opportunities that fit school needs and write proposals that benefit each other.

A Community-Based Partnership Program

While the focus should be in-house partnerships, reaching out the community as a partner can benefit the home team. In most areas, schools are a vital part of the community—and are locally controlled. While the traditional premise that schools educate the future local community doesn't hold as much weight now, certainly students interact *now* in the community and should access local expertise. And the community surely benefits when it accesses current knowledge in education. As the library shares its program, several worthwhile activities can be enhanced through community partnerships.

Collection development
- Donations of materials can be culled from bookstores, local agencies, and libraries.
- Peer school libraries, as well as other types of libraries, can share resources through interlibrary loan and collaborative Web pages.

Information literacy
- Share or adapt learning aids from other libraries.
- Team-teach literacy skills for the school community and the community at large.
- Work with local cable companies to produce information literacy videos.

Reading encouragement
- Start community-based book clubs.
- Give workshops on book selection for children.
- Train students to tell stories at local day care centers.
- Sponsor writing workshops for the community.
- Host bookstore events.
- Help youth groups with reading-related activities.

Programs and events
- Co-sponsor speakers.
- Present library-related topics at local clubs. Join relevant clubs.
- Include the library as part of a community event.
- Host town meetings on library-related topics such as Internet use or intellectual freedom.

Products
- Co-produce videos on community issues.
- Contribute library-related articles for local publications.
- Help design Web sites for local nonprofit organizations.
- Produce book lists for local groups.
- Provide background research information for community agencies and legislators on school-related topics.

Fund raising
- Seek sponsorship or contributions from local businesses for library events open to the public.
- Publicize and support local fund-raising efforts.
- Offer space for community fund-raising activities.

Here is one example of an outreach workshop:

SAMPLE WORKSHOP: Encouraging Your Child To Read

INTENDED AUDIENCE: Parents of children in elementary grades.

OBJECTIVES: Parents will list ways they can help their children enjoy reading and identify book selection tools.

SET-UP: Arrange parents in small groups by child's grade level for guided practice. Display resources on the tables for parents to browse. Use a large newsprint pad on an easel, presentation software, or overhead transparencies to present information. Supple each group with newsprint or clear transparency to "publish" its ideas and writing materials to take notes.

WORKSHOP OVERVIEW: 145 minutes

Introduction:	Welcome, housekeeping details, directions	10
Rationale:	Why involve parents?	15
Activities:	Selecting books	15
	Reading with your child	15
	Group processing	10
Break:		10
Resources:	Bibliography	10
Planning	Small groups plan reading activities	30
	Report out and processing	10
Wrap-up:	Summary, assessment, follow-up	15

EARLY BIRD ACTIVITY:
- Hand out Reading Encouragement Checklist (follows).
- Display resources on tables for parents to browse.

INTRODUCTION:
- Post the agenda and state the goals clearly so parents will know what to expect.
- Emphasize resource-based learning and parent-librarian collaboration.

RATIONALE:
- Have parents in pairs review the checklist.
- Have each pair report one insight about their children's reading. Record their findings.
- Point out that parents are the single most important factor in a child's reading habits and that children establish their reading patterns in the elementary school years. Even illiterate parents can share picture books with their children. They can listen to their children read. They can share stories with their children. (If most children in the workshop are illiterate, share the book *Wednesday Surprise* with them.)
- State the importance of parental involvement in reading by saying, "As parents you are the most influential factors in your children's reading. And since reading is a significant factor in learning and in academic success, your involvement is a

powerful predictor of your child's success in the world. That you are here to learn how to encourage your child to read is the first step in doing so—and in ensuring your child's success in the real world."

ACTIVITIES: Begin this section by saying, "Let's see how reading can be encouraged. You have already shared insights from the Reading Encouragement Checklist. Now we are going to do a couple of activities that you might want to try at home. As we work through these exercises, I want you to reflect on these questions:

- What did you learn about reading?
- How did the activity facilitate reading?
- How can you encourage reading at home?

Feel free to make comments after each activity, or wait until this portion of the workshop is completed."

SELECTING BOOKS: This activity shows parents how to choose books for their children. Lead a group discussion on how parents choose books for their children. Record the parents' comments and insights. Illustrate points by showing relevant titles. Add to their ideas by noting:

- Children's comments from library sessions and peer opinions
- Book selection tools such as *Children's Catalog*
- Best book lists (noting that awards do not guarantee child interest)
- Parent guides such as Jim Trelease's *Read-Aloud Handbook* or the *New York Times Guide to Children's Reading*
- Book store recommendations (being mindful that parent appeal is not the same as child interest)

Suggest that a good book has

- Good plot and characterization
- Positive theme or message
- High quality illustrations (if a picture book)
- Nonsexist and nonracist perspective; avoids stereotypes
- Good binding

It appeals to your child's interests and challenges your child to read at a higher level. Tell the parents some good ways to buy books for their children:

- School library book fairs
- Public library book fairs
- School book clubs
- Commercial book clubs
- Bookstores that act as children's reading advocates

Remind parents that award-winners aren't always the best choices, that bookstores and book clubs don't have comprehensive collections, and that the final judge of a book's quality and appropriateness is the child. You may want to create a selection guide sheet from the above points.

READING WITH YOUR CHILD: Model a reading session by sharing a book aloud with parents. Simulate the family experience by having them sit closely and casually around you as you present the book. Discuss their response to the reading session. Synthesize their responses. Offer the following generalizations, perhaps in a guide sheet, about reading aloud to children:

- Sit close to the child.
- Let the child see the pictures and share the words with you.
- Short, frequent reading sessions are better than occasional long-winded sessions.
- Pace the story and vary your voice to hold interest.
- Read the entire book, or stop at an exciting climax point.
- Stop reading if the book is degrading, boring, or inaccurate.

- Allow time for the child to reflect and respond to the work.
- Share insights and responses.

Have each group reflect on the activity by answering the questions posed at the start of the session. Report their comments.

BREAK: Suggest that this time might be well spent examining book displays and parent shelves, since the next activity will be to construct a resource list of useful parent titles.

RESOURCES: Hand out a sample bibliography of parent sources for potential use at home. Show some titles that might otherwise be overlooked and suggest ways to use them at home.

PLANNING: Divide the large group into thirds and have them plan an activity with their children that will encourage reading. The groups may want to brainstorm a number of activities, but they should plan one activity in detail. Give them 10 minutes to summarize and record their plan and discuss the process they followed. They will then report to the large group. The resulting records may be typed up and distributed as a follow-up handout.

WRAP-UP: Summarize insights that the participants gained from planning ways to encourage reading at home. Each parent should walk away with at least one useable idea. Be sure the group is given at least five minutes to assess the workshop. This helps in planning future workshops. In closing, thank all the facilitators and participants.

RESOURCES: Annotated bibliographies of parent sources held by the library. The International Reading Association and the American Library Association have good materials.

ASSESSMENT: Each small group shares one idea for encouraging reading. The ideas may be typed up for follow-up distribution in school publications.

VARIATIONS: Focus on one type of activity: reading aloud, book selection. Modify sample activities to match different age levels of children.

READING ENCOURAGEMENT CHECKLIST

Directions: Check those activities you do to encourage your child's reading. Do you

- ☐ Read to your child?
- ☐ Read for your enjoyment?
- ☐ Teach your child nursery rhymes and alphabet songs?
- ☐ Listen to your child read?
- ☐ Talk about reading with your child?
- ☐ Relate stories to real-life experiences?
- ☐ Choose books with your child at the public libraries?
- ☐ Have your child attend children's programs at the public library?
- ☐ Buy your child books?
- ☐ Subscribe to children's magazines?
- ☐ Let your child choose books or magazines?
- ☐ Establish quiet times and places for home reading?
- ☐ Provide reading-related activities, such as reading games, shopping, doing activities that involve reading directions, or writing?
- ☐ Stimulate your child's interests by visiting museums, parks and historical sites?
- ☐ Encourage book exchanges between friends?
- ☐ Provide audiocassette or multimedia versions of books?
- ☐ Build links between television watching and reading?
- ☐ Look at reading-related Internet sites together?

(From *Workshops for Teachers*, pp. 133-136)

▶ POT TO PASTURE

The term "partnership" covers a wide range of relationships, from one-time bibliography creations to standing committee projects. The intensity and closeness of partnerships vary greatly, depending on personnel and tasks. To make it an equal partnership, both parties need to negotiate the level of skills, resources, time, and engagement.

Just as with friendships, different people need different amounts of "space" or intimacy. Some people like to connect daily or more often; others prefer a weekly e-mail check-in. Even the physical distance comfort level between people varies—from tactile reinforcement to across-the-table formality. Some people want to share their life histories in the process, while others prefer sticking to business. In addition, some people prefer to plunge into a project, working on it intensely, finishing it, and going onto to something else, while others enjoy an incremental approach over a longer period of time.

People's need for closeness can change over time. Typically, partnerships begin on a surface level as the two parties get to know one another and size up each other. As the comfort level grows, so does the depth of partnership. However, the pace of the growth may differ between the two people; one may want to collaborate daily, while the other may give the partnership a lower priority. In general, growth is dependent on the less intense person, since a perception of "pushiness" may drive the partnership apart.

To add to the complexity, the comfort level of "space" may change under certain circumstances. Under stress, some people need extra attention, while others want to be left alone. Even shifts in mood may call for a readjustment of space. Finding the balance between the needs of two parties requires sensitivity to body language as well as verbal cues: "Let's do lunch." "Tell me if I'm doing this right." "Let's carve out some serious time to work on this together." "I need some time to sort this out." "I'll get back to you." "I'm too tired to think about this now."

The nature of the task also defines the degree of partnership. Obviously, the larger and more complex the task, the greater the demand for partnering. A technology fair, for instance, requires much more planning, time, and attention to detail than a departmental session on subject-specific Web sites. In some cases, such as a speaker visit, partners may work in parallel rather than together as they would for, say, a videotape on oral presentation methods. New or open-ended tasks, such as establishing a tutoring service, may require lots of brainstorming, while maintenance tasks may focus on routine procedures such as managing a research Web page.

> In general, growth is dependent on the less intense person, since a perception of "pushiness" may drive the partnership apart.

On the concrete level, the task must match available resources and skills. The librarian with a strong collection can offer more opportunities for student research and more options for instructional partnerships. The librarian with technological skills will probably seem more credible as a partner for professional development. If a desired task such as videoconferencing demands resources and skills that a partner does not possess, then an alternative task will have to be considered, or the partners will have to focus first on acquiring those high-priority materials and competencies.

Time considerations also influence the degree of effort. For instance, applying for a grant with a two-week deadline may require urgent, intense effort, as opposed to guiding a reading initiative over the next two years. Time, in fact, can be the defining factor in the partnership. When can partners collaborate? Fortunately with telecommunications, this issue has become slightly less critical. Personal time, though, enters into the picture more. Depending on the party's time commitments outside of school (family, professional development, volunteer work, health), educational partnerships may have a lower priority.

In general, the more compatible the partners and the more significant the task and need for diverse resources and skills, the more meaningful the partnership.

▸ OBSTACLES AND INDUCEMENTS

Partnerships require conscious effort and support, and they are not always successful. Even with the best of intentions, partnerships can wither on the vine or sprout nasty weeds. With careful forethought and timely interventions, though, most partnerships can be satisfying and productive. Here are some of the factors to consider, and ways to work through them.

PERSONAL ISSUES. Entering into a partnership requires open willingness. People who don't feel self-confident and competent may think they have little to offer and fear that others will discover their limitations. Their potential partner can help them discover their own gifts. For such people, a short-term structured activity with immediate results can be a safe way to start a partnership.

Partners have to feel that they will benefit from the relationship. If one party thinks the other has little to offer or is unprofessional, then the relationship will be hard to maintain. The other party will have to prove personal worth, and that can be a draining task, especially at the start. Unless a partnership is forced upon one, it is better to focus on developing natural mutual goals and attractions. Then word of mouth can build the social or professional reputation that will make ensuing partnerships attractive.

Partnerships require risk-taking. Some people fear rejection. Others fear change. In either case, they are worried about leaving their comfort zone. The trick is to broaden that comfort zone so it doesn't seem so scary—or sacred. The easiest approach is to build on the partner's strengths, taking advantage of his areas of comfort. If the partner feels needed, he can help another person become more comfortable with a new skill or insight, and then that person may feel more willing to ask for help or learn from someone else.

> There should always be an "escape clause" if a partnership seems irreconcilable.

Partnerships can lead to commitment, which may threaten some people's need for flexibility or autonomy. To start with, tasks involving partnerships should probably have a starting and ending date so people can prepare themselves to stay the course if worse comes to worst. There should always be an "escape clause" if a partnership seems irreconcilable. After all, not every partnership is a good match—or, at least, that particular task might not work out. Taking a proactive stance, jointly developing a list of benefits when the partnership begins, and reviewing it during the task can frame the collaboration in a mutually satisfying way and can help build a solid foundation for longer-term partnerships.

Partnerships take work, plain and simple. That's why any collaborative effort should rise out of practical mutual need: No one person can do the job alone; no one person has all of the resources and skills to accomplish the task alone. Ideally, partnerships should exemplify the adage, "Work smarter, not harder." The work is easier if each party knows ahead what each person can contribute and how each one operates best. The fewer the unknowns, the fewer the worries and unpleasant surprises.

Hopefully, though, by working together, partners will learn more about one another and experience some positive surprises. Interestingly, partners actually nudge each other to perform at a higher level. So not only does the task achievement itself reflect a sum greater than its parts, but each partner may rise to a more professional level of effort. Effective partners realize each other's hard work and often give public recognition when no one else can appreciate the full extent of it.

SYSTEMIC ISSUES. Partnerships require resources, both human and material. Obviously, if the task requires resources that are not available, something has to change. Either the resources are found or the task must be modified. Sometimes a partner can suggest an alternative resource or task overlooked by the other party. Together, partners extend their networking circles to locate additional resources or find other people who have done similar tasks. The key is awareness of opportunities. For instance, if an author visit is cancelled at the last minute, then another speaker must be found. In this instance, a list of local authors is a must.

Time is usually seen as the big systemic obstacle: no time to collaborate or effect change. The real issue, though, is one of values. What does the school think important enough to carve out time for? In the business world, time is money. In the educational world, time is priority. Does the school value partnerships? Does the school value the particular task? The first question is a systemic one and must be confronted straightforwardly. The second question may be systemic, but is more likely one of individual awareness, and signals a need to educate those who do not see the worthiness of the task. If the task cannot be justified, then perhaps it shouldn't be done.

Partnerships are most fruitful if well supported by others and may die without support. Two or more people already committed to a task can enlist the support of their constituents. If one partner is not well known or supported by the other partner's network, the "halo effect" of being accepted by the partner should improve that person's reputation and ease the way for support by the other group. In that way, support can grow from a grassroots effort to be incorporated eventually into the school's support system.

> Recognition is a mindset that needs to be shared.

Partnerships need to be recognized. There's nothing more demoralizing than to work hard to accomplish a task in the hopes of improving the school and have no one recognize or adopt the effort.

While administrators still represent the most influential source of recognition, partners need to boost each other and to use their own influence to find ways to recognize and take advantage of the fruits of their labor. Have colleagues pilot-test the partners' project and give feedback. Provide opportunities for professional development such as individual coaching. Communicate the efforts and impact through newsletters, meetings, and word of mouth. Make sure that achievements are woven into school reports. Thank partners, and support other partnerships. Recognition is a mindset that needs to be shared.

WHEN CONFLICTS ARISE. Partners don't have to enjoy each other's company socially, although it helps. The most important considerations are respectful professional courtesy and the ability to carry out the task at hand. Preventive measures are the best approach, of course: establishing a climate of trust. Still, conflicts do occur and need to be resolved.

Individuals react differently to a situation based on a number of factors:

- Values: what people find important and right,
- Needs: what people need and want,
- Goals: people's objectives and task identification,
- Methods: strategies people use to act, and
- Facts: what people know or how they interpret the facts.

When those factors influence action that runs counter to a partner's values, needs, goals, methods, and perceptions, then conflicts are likely. If one person values detailed organization and the other one dismisses that value, then work habits may lead to conflict.

Understanding these underlying differences, the parties need to identify and own the problem. Whose problem is it? In some cases, a person may approach a task in a way that discomforts the other party. If the task can be done successfully that way, then the uncomfortable person has the problem and must decide if he can tolerate the differing method. In other cases, the problem may be mutual or may adversely affect others, so it needs to be solved by both partners.

As alternative solutions are suggested, both parties must speak clearly, listen closely to each other, and consider emotional content as well as data. Each person's working style must be appreciated and integrated into the plan. For instance, the visionary should be praised for seeing the big picture, and the detail person needs to be valued for fine-tuning the solution. The naysayer may need solid evidence to justify trust. In general, once the motive for a person's attitude and behavior is determined, then the partners can deal with ways to satisfy that person's needs and accomplish the task at hand.

▶ THE IMPACT OF TECHNOLOGY

Just think about the impact that technology has had on gardening and agriculture: the plow, the combine, irrigation. Technology has the potential to impact partnerships as well. No longer need partnerships be constrained by space and time. Committee work is often conducted "in real time" solely through telecommunications: telephone, groupware, chat rooms and videoconferencing. Work can also be accomplished asynchronously through e-mail and other threaded "conversations." Fax technology speeds up response time and delivers a quality product. School community members can meet online without leaving their respective rooms or residences.

> These days, the task, more than the physical realities, determines the partnership.

Partnerships can be composed of experts throughout the world as easily as within one district, expanding the potential for interaction and novel ideas.

These days, the task, more than the physical realities, determines the partnership. Technology lends itself to the creative process. Authors now co-write books without ever meeting face to face. Committees develop policies and guidelines by building on each other's thoughts electronically. Even professional development can be done by planning and implementing the content and delivery system electronically. Distance learning through videoconferencing and Web-based instruction has become commonplace.

On the other hand, in-house instructional partnerships usually require face-to-face work.

Physical proximity is certainly desirable. Technology is a more abstract and artificial way to communicate.

Indeed, the social aspect of the partnership may feel more constrained in "virtual," electronically defined partnerships. The term "high tech, high touch" applies here. Rather than dismiss or limit technological partnerships, people need to find ways to incorporate social aspects in the electronic picture. Regardless of the medium, partners need to get to know one another. In the cyber world, this may be done through sharing personal Web pages, taking more time to chat online, or creating videoconferencing opportunities. Because nonverbal cues are usually missing, compensatory methods must come into play: videotaping oneself in action, telling personal stories, sharing best practices. Some technology-based partners meet in person at the beginning to establish that personal touch, and then reconvene as needed, say annually. The quality of interaction, the significance of the task, and the time frame all influence the degree of personalization and physical presence needed to support the partnership.

HOW DOES THE PARTNERSHIP GARDEN GROW?

While it is possible to maintain partnerships *pro forma*, assessment enables partnerships to reach their full potential. In fact, the issue of assessment should be addressed when a partnership is established: "What do we want to accomplish, and how will we know if we accomplished it or not?" Partners need to determine what to measure, how to measure it, who will measure it, and when and where it will be measured. Then they need to determine how to use the assessment once it is made, or it is of little value.

In each case, partners address the following issues:

- The activity or service,
- The results or impact of the activity or service,
- The process,
- The underlying partnership, and
- The partners themselves.

Typically, a baseline assessment should be done at the start to measure eventual progress. Formative assessment enables partners to modify direction and strategy along the way. Summative assessment provides the final opportunity to determine the significance of the task and partnership as well as the need for follow-up work.

As to the question of what to measure, here are several factors to consider:

Participation:
- How many partnerships have been established?
- What partnerships meet regularly?
- How long-standing are those partnerships?
- How substantial are the partnerships?
- Is there a sense of "our" library?
- Are teachers there when librarians need them?

Planning:
- What kinds of decisions are made by partners?
- Do partners share equally in planning and implementation?
- Are partners dependable and thorough?
- Is planning done effectively and productively?
- Do plans accurately reflect school needs?
- What is the quality of resultant plans?

Interpersonal relationships:
- Do partners respect and trust each other?
- Are partners able to accept and negotiate differences?
- Do partners support each other and their plans?

Results:
- What effect did the activity or product have?
- What help and what hindered positive results?
- What should be changed and what should be continued?
- How did the results affect the partnership?

Assessment should look at both the objective and subjective factors in partnerships. Personal affinities and conflicts need to the acknowledged and dealt with; one partner may be a "nice person" but a lousy planner. Sometimes tasks can be successfully planned and implemented with little personal agreement. Likewise, great friendships may exist between librarians and other personnel with no transfer to effective practice. All kinds of partnerships are viable and should be recognized and nurtured. All can benefit, ultimately and most importantly, the students.

Because educational partnerships are so complicated, a good way to look at the total picture is to develop a portfolio of evidence, a collection of documents that shows the partners' plans, progress, and results. A typical portfolio would include surveys, focus group notes, lesson plans, products (of the partners and the students), documentation of events and displays (photos, videos, flyers), copies of library-aided student research projects, and user statistics. This evidence can be sorted and analyzed from several standpoints, depending on the goal of the assessment.

For all assessments, the most important steps are analysis and resultant action. What patterns emerge from the data, and why? What differences do the results make? Can anything be changed? Assessment is most effective when it leads to needed change. Partners can get at the underlying problem and offer solutions.

When implementing solutions, which usually means changing some factor, partners should consider

Time frame of the problem and solution:
- Are short-term solutions sufficient?
- Is the problem a matter of graduating students?
- Can the solution wait or is immediate action required?

People involved:
- Can library staff solve the problem?
- Who needs to change?
- Who needs to decide about change?
- Which personnel will retire or be hired?

Perceptions:
- Is the library the problem, and does it need to change?
- Are people unaware of the library program, and do they need to be educated?
- Are underlying systems obstacles to good library programs, and do they need to be changed?

Regardless of the results, the assessment needs to be communicated to relevant parties. Suggestions should be acted upon immediately, at least at a token level, if only for image-building. Those who help with the assessment need to know that their input makes a difference; even the smallest, tangible change will demonstrate that the people in power listened and responded. This kind of consideration will build more partnerships than a myriad newsletters or smiles.

The following rubric offers a guide:

> Personal affinities and conflicts need to the acknowledged and dealt with; one partner may be a "nice person" but a lousy planner.

LIBRARIAN (LMT) PARTNERSHIP RUBRIC

ACTIVITY	EXEMPLARY	GOOD	FAIR	LIMITED
ASSESSMENT	Partners use various assessment strategies to evaluate students/services. Assessment drives curricular program. Assessment is used to improve resources/instruction.	Partners regularly assess students/services. Assessment informs curricular program. Assessment informs resources/instruction decisions.	LMT or partner sometimes assesses students/services. Assessment sometimes impacts curricular or instructional decisions.	Partners do not share assessments. Assessments seldom inform curriculum decisions.
PLANNING	LMT is full curriculum development partner. Full range of info lit skills are integrated in curriculum. All activities involving the library are planned cooperatively. LMT is involved throughout planning process.	LMT helps develop curriculum. Most info lit skills are integrated into curriculum. Many activities involving the library are planned cooperatively. LMT plays significant role in planning.	LMT supports curriculum development. Some info lit skills are integrated into curriculum. Some activities involving the library are planned cooperatively. LMT plays a limited role in planning.	LMT follows curriculum development. A few info lit skills are integrated—or are taught in isolation. Few activities involving the library are planned cooperatively. LMT isn't part of plan.
IMPLEMENTATION	Partners usually team-teach. Partners use a variety of strategies and resources. Partners assess student achievement regularly. Partners modify plan as needed in collaboration with others.	Partners sometimes team-teach. Partners share several strategies and resources. Partners sometimes assess student achievement. Partners make some plan changes as needed.	Partners decide who teaches. Partners share some resources or strategies. Partners assess student achievement unevenly. Partners occasionally change plans.	LMT doesn't teach. Resources and strategies aren't shared. LMT does not access student work. Partners seldom change plans.
COMMITMENT	Partners communicate regularly with each other and with the school community. Partnership is long term and close. Peer coaching is ubiquitous.	Partners communicate regularly with each other. Partners have worked together and coached each other regularly.	Partners sometimes communicate and work together, usually for short-term activities. Peer coaching is spotty.	Partners seldom communicate, coach or work with each other. Activities are one time only.

A framework for a partnership portfolio would typically include the following types of evidence (in accord with AASL's *Information Power*):

Learning and teaching:
- Scope and sequence of information literacy skills,
- Rubrics as assessment tools,
- Sample lesson plans,
- Videos of instructional sessions,
- Learning aids for technology,
- Reader advisory lists,
- IEPs with specifics about library use, and
- sample student work incorporating technology

Information access and delivery:
- Instructional aids,
- Diagram of physical facility,
- Monthly schedule,
- Minutes of library council meetings, and
- Policy on challenged materials, policies.

Program administration:
- Library mission statement,
- Staff list,
- Library long-range plan,
- School community survey of library services,
- Sample workshop outline,
- Library publications, and
- Library budget.

Each year the librarian may wish to focus on specific elements of the library media program, as this one-year professional goals statement does:

Encourage reading:
- Displays
- Talk about books with teachers and students
- Establish book discussion club
- Work with English department on book discussion
- Sponsor reading and book events

Assessment: teacher and student feedback, book circulation, event or club participation

Advance information literacy:
- Participate in research strategies study group
- Revise research handbook
- Instruct students in Internet and online use

Assessment: documents for group, teacher and student feedback, meeting minutes, schedule, products, evaluation of student research reports

Work with target groups:
- Coordinate with special education department
- Get materials for ESL students

Assessment: schedule list, book lists, visits with special education teachers, group feedback

Advance technology:
- Chair site technology committee
- Participate in district technology committee
- Index and make Web sites available to departments
- Develop a research Web page

Assessment: meeting minutes, documents, Web site, teacher and student feedback

▶ LIFE CYCLES OF PARTNERSHIPS

Partnerships are not static. Like other relationships, they grow, mature, and change. Even long-standing partnerships may change because of changing roles in the school community, personal changes, and the interplay of personalities. Recognizing those metamorphoses eases the necessary shifts and affirms the underlying nature of the partnerships.

IN THE BEGINNING. Starting partnerships requires—and fosters—quick energy coupled with caution. A specific activity with a set time frame and immediate results improves the odds of initial success. A one-shot lesson plan is typical. This is a time of testing personality combinations, teamwork, trust, and dependability. That first impression forms the foundation for long-term relationships, not just one-time efforts.

CREATING NORMS. As the partnership grows, each party negotiates acceptable roles and behaviors. What are the limits? What are the possibilities? A sense of guardedness still surrounds the partnership as each member determines how much is at stake in the long run. This scenario is especially true in beginning partnerships between a school librarian and a department. What is needed to maintain the partnership? What personal behaviors or attitudes must change? What benefits will result?

DEALING WITH CONFLICT. As the partnership matures, the masks of convention may fall and conflicts may arise. This is actually a healthy state, one in which the partners feel they can be honest. It is also a make or break point in that how conflicts are resolved—or dodged—determines the depth and durability of the partnership. For instance, if the partner can't handle criticism, then the relationship will have to retreat a bit and assume a more transient or sensitive nature. If, on the other hand, those conflicted issues can be successfully resolved, the partnership will likely be more durable and accomplish more significant work. Substantial projects such as school self-studies exemplify this stage.

MATURE PARTNERSHIPS. In a well-developed and sustained partnership, each partner accommodates the other as needed. There is a large comfort zone in which to maneuver, and limits are well defined. At this point, other people usually join the partnership. Partners feel comfortable bringing others to the fold, mentoring them in the process. Long-term mentoring programs are an interesting version of this type of partnership.

REFRAMING THE PARTNERSHIP. If new ideas and activities aren't incorporated into the partnership, it may grow rigid or stale. Like a marriage, partnerships require constant maintenance. In some cases, outside forces may redefine the partnership. For instance, one partner may become a department chair and need to spend more time establishing mentoring relationships. A partner may feel the need to go in a new direction to refresh his educational commitment, and seek other partners. Curriculum may change. A partner may be undergoing personal changes in lifestyle or family commitments. Both internal and external forces can change the equilibrium of the partnership at any time. The key is to reframe the partnership so it can be sustained at some level and benefit both sides.

> Like a marriage, partnerships require constant maintenance.

Where Do Partners Practice?

*To get started, you must have a destination.
You become successful the moment you start moving
toward a worthwhile goal.*

The real test of partnerships is in their implementation and impact on the learning community. Do they make a difference? *Information Power* is predicated on the need for partnerships in order to provide high-quality library programs. Indeed, focusing on student learning, it presupposes that the librarian needs to collaborate with the entire school to ensure student achievement outside the library as well. In this picture of school-wide learning, the librarian brings unique contributions and operates within certain delineated parameters. In this way, the librarian truly complements the rest of the school, strengthening the overall effort.

The new AASL document also provides a working structure for examining and assessing practice. This chapter delineates principles of a good library program and furnishes examples of good practice from simple day-to-day collaboration to systemic reform. The focus is on librarian-teacher partnerships. However, other collaborations with students, support staff, parents, and the community also make up the library media program.

▶ INFORMATION LITERACY STANDARDS

A basic goal of the library program is to ensure that students will be effective idea and information users. Toward that goal, the American Association of School Librarians has promulgated standards for information literacy. Each of these standards can be reached through meaningful partnerships. Examples follow:

Standard 1: Accessing information efficiently and effectively. Teachers can work with librarians to provide learning experiences that foster information access, such as teaching methods of accessing magazine indexes both in hard copy and online; instructing students in techniques of using online library catalogs; creating Webliographies that identify likely sources.

Standard 2: Evaluating information. The librarian can teach Internet navigation and Web site assessment in computer literacy classes.

Standard 3: Using information accurately and creatively. The librarian can work with the computer specialist to train students in using multimedia authoring tools to present their research findings.

Standard 4: Pursuing information related to personal interests. The librarian can work with club advisors to provide materials that support the clubs' agendas.

Standard 5: Appreciating literature and other creative expressions. The librarian can work with the drama department to help students find stories to dramatize.

Standard 6: Striving for information seeking and knowledge generation. The librarian can work with the classroom teacher to provide learning experiences such as debates and simulations.

Standard 7: Recognizing the importance of information to a democracy. The librarian can help social issues teachers and special interest clubs to act politically based on research.

Standard 8: Practicing ethical behavior in regard to information *and its technology.* As an assignment planned by the librarian and classroom teacher, students develop a code of ethics for dealing with information technology.

Standard 9: Participating in groups to pursue and generate information. Teachers and librarian determine the social and academic tasks that students need to demonstrate. Teacher-librarian lesson plans model collaborative efforts.

Librarian-teacher partnerships usually focus on helping students become information literate, but they should also encourage students to use information for personal reasons—and for fun.

As librarians, in partnership with teachers, examine each standard, they need to make several decisions:

- At what point in the student's development should each competency be introduced, mastered, reinforced, or reviewed? Grade level might not be the best determinant; readiness varies greatly even within the same age group. Ideally, individualized or small group lesson plans let students learn at their own pace.

- In what subject areas should competency be couched? Perhaps one subject or learning unit is particularly appropriate for presenting a concept. In other cases, a skill may be introduced in a variety of ways or disciplines, permitting reinforcement of the competency.

- What roles do librarians and other educators play in teaching each competency? As the planning process and partnerships improve, this question becomes easier to answer.

Librarians can approach information literacy instruction via department or grade level, or the scope can be interdepartmental and intergrade. For example, a school might choose "rain forests" as a unifying theme, the librarian working with teachers to plan age-appropriate lessons. The results of the students' inquiries and research can be displayed throughout the school and shared during an open house. Other themes that lend themselves to schoolwide partnerships include historical periods, human subgroups, astronomy, the arts, seasons and holidays, sports, living things, literary forms, and social issues.

A typical approach might involve presentation of general reference tools in tandem with

> ...They should also encourage students to use information for personal reasons— and for fun.

specific strategies based on topic. Alternatively, librarians may pose trivia questions at the beginning of a unit to expose students to specialized references. After instruction, the librarian can provide guidance on materials as students need them. A third alternative might focus on a subject's application to the real world. Using mathematics as an example, librarians might pose questions about cooking or economics that can be answered by using library references.

Here is a suggested sequence of activities that covers information literacy competencies. As with all aspects of the educational program, it can become richer through partner planning.

Primary Grades

Access:
- Find your way through a book.
- Find pictures of families in picture books.
- Alphabet soup: find books by author.
- Follow a story on an audiocassette.

Evaluation:
- Is the book too hard for me?
- What do pictures tell us?
- What fits in this story? What doesn't?

Information use:
- Play a game based on a story.
- Make character puppets.
- Create a radio show from audio sources.

Personal:
- Find a source about a favorite pet.
- Read a story about a family who moves.

Appreciation:
- Dance to poetry rhythm.
- Act out stories.
- Make posters from favorite fairy tales.

Knowledge generation:
- Make a personal time line.
- Create a scrapbook about the community from found items and student work.

Sharing knowledge:
- Present a skit to local government about water conditions.
- Send a photo album about the school to another school.

Upper Elementary

Access:
- Map encyclopedia cross-references.
- Develop word trees using the dictionary.
- Find video clips on a topic.

Evaluation:
- Compare dictionaries and encyclopedias.
- Compare two movies about a topic.
- Compare fiction and nonfiction treatments of history.
- Determine facts and opinions in a science article.

Information use:
- Write other endings to stories.
- Trace changing boundaries over time.
- Make a storyboard about a famous person.

Personal:
- Find joke books.
- Find out why dinosaurs became extinct.
- Use a book or video to make dolls.

Appreciation:
- Dress up as a literary character.
- Hold a reading contest.
- Use the *BookWhiz* database.

Knowledge generation:
- Create original folktales.
- Produce a play about a historical event.
- Create a game based on a story.

Sharing knowledge:
- Videotape community agencies.
- Make an audiotape of an interview with an older relative.

Middle School

Access:
- Use magazine indexes for class speeches.
- Conduct energy surveys.
- Use a CD-ROM encyclopedia to find maps.

Evaluation:
- Compare two magazine articles about a current issue.
- Compare men's and women's sports rules.
- Determine the authority of a Web site.

Information use:
- Extrapolate social values from myths.
- Identify plants using nature guides.
- Trace a day via the newspaper.
- Determine how movies portray different ethnic groups.

Personal:
- Find soccer techniques.
- Read about acne.
- Find out how to draw horses.

Appreciation:
- Create a shadow puppet show based on a fable.
- Review books.
- Make a hypermedia stack about a favorite story.

Knowledge generation:
- Create a visual dictionary.
- Build a scale model.
- Create comic books on topics.

Sharing knowledge:
- Become a storyteller.
- Produce a school news show.

High School

Access:
- Use poetry indexes to locate poems by subject.
- Use online Boolean searching to find subject matter.
- Use almanacs to find economic trends.
- E-mail science experts.

Evaluation:
- Compare primary and secondary sources.
- Examine magazine and Internet advertisements for social messages.
- Analyze propaganda posters.
- Compare different types of maps.
- Identify bogus Web sites.

Information use:
- Extrapolate science from science fiction.
- Analyze career representations in fiction and nonfiction.
- Interpret psychological problems in television shows using different schools of psychology.
- Study history from the Native American perspective.
- Chart AIDS distribution.

Personal:
- Locate laws about student rights.
- Research the most appropriate college for you.
- Find out how to write a resume.
- Make natural cosmetics.
- Learn how to program.

Appreciation:
- Start a book discussion group.
- Write reviews on the school's Web page.
- Produce a student literary CD-ROM.
- Produce a slide-tape show on Mexican masks and music.

Knowledge generation:
- Create mock interviews with historic figures.
- Debate issues.
- Develop hypermedia files on biodiversity.
- Produce a visual essay on prejudice.

Sharing knowledge:
- Develop a heritage hike.
- Start a tutoring service.
- Write legislation.

The following lesson plan exemplifies teacher-librarian planning:

SUPREME COURT SIMULATION LESSON PLAN

ACTIVITY DESCRIPTION: Students present Constitutional case issues before a mock Supreme Court.

CONTENT OUTCOMES: Students will:
- Interpret Constitutional case issues in light of precedents.
- Identify typical judgments of Supreme Court justices.
- Debate a Constitutional case, either in defense or prosecution.

INFORMATION LITERACY OUTCOMES: Students will:
- Access information from a variety of sources about Constitutional case issues and Supreme Court justices (Standard 1).
- Evaluate information to verify facts and determine perspectives (Standard 2).
- Synthesize and organize findings into a legal argument (Standards 3, 6, 7).
- Critique performance based on interpreting video footage (Standard 2).

PREREQUISITE SKILLS:
- Use reference tools to access sources.
- Videotape (optional).
- Use debate techniques.

TEACHER PREPARATION:
- Design case studies.
- Designate justices (optional).
- Determine cooperative groups (optional).
- Introduce activity to class.

LIBRARIAN PREPARATION:
- Gather resources.
- Bookmark Web sites.
- Develop "pathway" to help students find relevant sources.
- Instruct students on use of government sources.
- Provide videotaping equipment and camera crew (or train students in videotaping).

GROUP ACTIVITY:
1. Nine students choose a Supreme Court justice. Write a profile on the justice and his or her decisions. Choose a Chief Justice among the group.
2. In groups of threes, students research a case, drawing on the Constitutional issues and precedents.
3. As a group, decide whether to defend or prosecute the case. One student will be principal writer; one will act as presenting lawyer. Separately, the justice member of the group will draw up at least three questions for the lawyer.
4. Hold a mock Supreme Court hearing. Justices in black robes hear the cases, which are videotaped.
5. Justices discuss and debate the issue and the Chief Justice writes the decision. The others submit individual decisions.
6. Lawyers submit their speeches and notes. Writers submit research on Constitutional issues and precedents.
7. All students write a self-evaluation based on their experiences and their critiques of their performances on videotape.

ASSESSMENT:
- Teacher assesses students' arguments and support in terms of accuracy, thoroughness, and clarity.
- Librarian assesses students' research in terms of accuracy, thoroughness, and appropriateness.

▶ TEACHING AND LEARNING

The heart of education is learning: interacting with ideas and changing as a result. Partners promote information literacy and diversity, model collaboration, incorporate technology, and frame curriculum effectively. These are all pro-active measures to ensure that students will have opportunities to construct knowledge and connect it with other information both within the realm of the school and beyond. Each principle of school library media programs addresses these processes and calls for professional partnerships.

INTEGRATE THE LIBRARY MEDIA PROGRAM. In the past, the library was sometimes "in the school but not of the school." Students were sent to the library during the teacher's prep period to hear stories and check out books. No longer. Student learning is now the center of the school, and staff and services need to be choreographed to optimize educational experiences. How do students get their hands on resources? How do they learn how to manipulate them? How do they interpret and make them their own? Neither the classroom teacher nor the librarian can do it alone. Instead, collaborative effort needs to guide student learning.

While teachers tend to know their subject areas in depth, they often do not have a strong handle on the variety of current materials in their field. Nor do they tend to make connections with resources in related areas. That's where the librarian can help, showing students specialized resources and access tools to relevant information. Working across the curriculum, the librarian actually has a greater ability than most teachers to help students make those cognitive connections across subjects. Knowing how a bird flies can help a student understand how planes work. Understanding Hindu religion can help one interpret Indian paintings. Knowledge of mythology can increase vocabulary.

The librarian may notice that students can't find magazine articles because they don't know how to use a periodicals index. Integrating that skill into the curriculum makes the students more successful. Perhaps students don't know how to navigate the Internet and so do not learn about current trends in some social issue. That information skill can be taught in another class, even in a computer literacy course, and then applied in academic coursework. In effect, the librarian is helping to tie curriculum together so all teachers and students can benefit.

> Working across the curriculum, the librarian actually has a greater ability than most teachers to help students make those cognitive connections across subjects.

When teachers design learning activities or develop curriculum, do they think about the library? They should. But it won't happen if successful projects aren't visible or if the librarian isn't involved, preferably from the start. In terms of school structure, the librarian needs to find out how instructional decisions are made and participate in those forums. Is the librarian a department chair? Does he head curriculum task forces? Is he a leader in school reform? Even if the librarian plays a background role by providing needed research or publicizing efforts on the library Web page, concrete contributions demonstrate knowledge and competence and keep the librarian in the loop.

INTEGRATE INFORMATION LITERACY STANDARDS. Remember the era of "It's Tuesday, so it must be *Reader's Guide* day"? Just as reading and writing permeate the curriculum, so does information literacy. Indeed, information literacy is actually a more profound concept than either reading or writing because it addresses *all* kinds of ways people take in information, process it, and share it. So it is not just the responsibility of the librarian to teach those skills. Rather, the entire school needs to provide opportunities for students to learn and practice those competencies. Not only does this entail working with teachers to craft assignments that address those skills, but it also means that librarians need to train teachers in those competencies and ways to help others learn them.

Some teacher preparation programs still do not focus on information literacy, so entering professionals may not know what those skills are or how to teach them. It's all too easy to say, "The librarian will take care of that," but teachers need to know enough about the process to work with their students in research projects. Especially since learning is not room-bound, when students ask questions about processing information in class, teachers need to be able to answer competently then and there. And librarians need to help teachers gain those skills, even if it means just making sure that the teacher listens to literacy instruction when students come to the library for research.

Librarians, too, need to keep abreast of information literacy skills. Twenty years ago there was no Internet (although its predecessor was used in government and research settings); "surfing the Net" would have been meant "surfing with a net" to a beach boy. As tools have become more sophisticated and information itself has proliferated, librarians need to constantly update and expand their own information literacy skills. And as more is known about how people learn, librarians need to incorporate that research in their instruction. Thus, librarian-teacher partnerships help both parties learn from each other and compound their efforts to support student achievement.

Ideally, the entire school should work together to integrate information literacy standards throughout the curriculum.

- What competencies should all students be able to demonstrate when they matriculate?
- At what level should those skills be introduced, reviewed, and mastered? And what constitutes mastery?
- What opportunities should be made available for students to learn and practice those skills?
- How can efforts in one class be transferred to another class?

When the entire school community can agree on the answers to those questions and share the responsibility for ensuring that students meet the standards, then learning will be optimized and no one person will feel burdened with that critical task.

> It's all too easy to say, "The librarian will take care of that," but teachers need to know enough about the process to work with their students in research projects.

PROCESS	RESEARCH SKILLS INSTRUCTION / SKILL	MS	9TH	10TH	11TH	12TH
PLAN	task defined		English	English	English	English
	thesis/question/hypothesis			Science		
	cooperative group role defined		Math	Math		
ACCESS	use of library catalog	■				
	sections of library	■				
	use of search/key words	■				
	dictionary/encyclopedia/almanac	■				
	Reader's Guide		Social Studies			
	computer indexes		Social Studies			
	CD-ROM	■				
	online resources (Internet, e-mail)		Applied Tech			
	search strategies			English		
	specialized references			Science		
	specialized indexes			Science		
	Interviews			English		
EVALUATE	main ideas	Social Studies				
	compare sources on same topic	Social Studies				
	point of view/fact vs. opinion	Social Studies				
	visual literacy		Arts			
	graph interpretation		Science	Science		
	numerical analysis		Math	Math		
	content analysis		English	English	English	English
	primary vs. secondary sources		Social Studies	Social Studies	Social Studies	Social Studies
	quality of info (credibility)		Social Studies	Social Studies	Social Studies	Social Studies
	Internet sources		Applied Tech			
	use of rubrics		English	English	English	English
	research process			Science		
	research product			Science		
ORGANIZE	notetaking	■				
	summarizing	■				
	classifying		Science			
	sequencing (timeline)	■				
	format appropro to info		Applied Tech			
	research paper format			English		
	use of graphic organizer		Science	Science		
	outlining	■				
	visual elements		Arts			
	bibliography	■				
	annotated bibliography		Social Studies			
	footnotes/citations		Social Studies			
	no plagiarism					
PRODUCE	2-D product (poster, collage)		Arts			
	oral report		English	English	English	English
	skit/play/demo		Arts			
	video product		Arts			
	critical review		English	English	English	English
	research paper		Science			
	I-search paper			English		
	computer product (non wp)		Applied Tech			

PROMOTE COLLABORATIVE PLANNING AND CURRICULUM DEVELOPMENT. Surprisingly, collaboration among teachers is not ubiquitous. Sometimes the closest to sharing is passing the VCR/TV cart between classrooms. Even some teacher preparation programs do not dwell on educational partnerships, sad to say. Therefore, librarians are often models of collaboration. Fortunately, because librarians work with all students and all teachers across the curriculum, they are in a perfect situation to "lead from the middle."

Especially if teachers operate in relative isolation, they often do not realize that assignments from other disciplines may overlap. Indeed, even within the same department, different courses may include similar assignments. Both a foreign language and a world cultures teacher may have students develop travel brochures on a French-speaking country, for example. The librarian can inform each teacher, as well as suggest that the project count for both classes or that each teacher take a different approach to the project.

Suppose a teacher wants students to create a *PowerPoint* presentation on a political campaign. Coordination is needed among the classroom teacher, librarian, and technology specialist. If students don't know how to use that authoring tool, then that skill must be taught. Both the instructor and the site for instruction must be scheduled. Students might not know how to find current information on politics, so the librarian needs to determine the site, instruction, and resources to teach those skills. Perhaps some students have technological skills. If so, then collaborative grouping may be most effective, and the classroom teacher may have to play choreographer, rotating students to different rooms for different activities.

Librarians used to be more in the business of physical access to information rather than intellectual access and processing. Now librarians bring to the table information literacy objectives to match and coordinate with the classroom teacher's content and objectives. Together, the teacher and librarian can plan and carry out the activities (both teaching and learning) and provide the resources (both material and human) needed. Both can assess the process and product of students—and themselves. This one-unit approach can be broadened to encompass long-term coordination and, ultimately, the whole curriculum design and implementation.

Imagine the power of cooperatively creating a seamless course of learning experiences combining content and process, determining optimum resources, making sure those resources are available when needed, and providing authentic assessment of constructive knowledge! The following is one such example:

> Fortunately, because librarians work with all students and all teachers across the curriculum, they are in a perfect situation to "lead from the middle."

EXAMPLE: HISPANIC PAINTERS

PARTNERS: Library media teacher, Spanish language teacher, art teacher, computer specialist. The partners must

DEFINE THE AUDIENCE: Students
- What are their needs in terms of information? Details about Hispanic painters, Spanish, picture scanning techniques, Web page design
- What experience do they have that can help shape learning? Spanish fluency, knowledge about painters and painting, locational skills, scanning, and Web page design skills
- What do they need to know ahead of time, or prepare ahead for? Spanish

CLARIFY THE OBJECTIVE: Facilitate student learning
- Content objective: Describe and critique Hispanic painters and their work in Spanish
- Information literacy objective: Locate information about Hispanic painters, transform findings into Web page format
- Social objective: Divide responsibilities fairly
- Assessment: Project rubric, evaluation of written fluency, evaluation of artistic analysis

NEGOTIATE THE CONTENT:
- What information competencies will be addressed? Locational skills, Web page design
- What aspects of the subject area will be covered? Hispanic painters, art analysis

DETERMINE WHAT RESOURCES WILL BE USED:
- Library: Print, nonprint, and digital sources, computer workstations with scanners
- Computer lab: Computer workstations with scanners
- Availability: Need to schedule rooms

DETERMINE THE DELIVERY SYSTEM(S):
- Format: Lecture, learning stations
- Support materials to produce: Scanning directions, handout on Web page design (by computer specialist)

DETERMINE THE TIME FRAME: One-time project scheduled for one week

DECIDE LOCATION: Two days in the library, two days in the computer lab, one day in class (schedule ahead)

DECIDE WHO WILL TEACH OR PRESENT THE INFORMATION:
- How will instructional duties be determined? By expertise
- Will more than one person be involved? All partners—art teacher for art analysis, Spanish teacher for biography, librarian for locational skills and technology, computer specialist for Web and scanning

DESIGN THE LEARNING ACTIVITY:
- When and where will student practice occur? In library and computer lab
- Will students work independently or in groups? Collaborative groups of three
- Will homework be assigned? Outside time may be needed to complete project
- What standards of performance and supervision will be required? Rubrics for project, art analysis, Spanish fluency, information skills

PLAN HOW TO ASSESS THE ACTIVITY:
- What will be assessed? The plan, the delivery, the activity itself, the results
- Who will be assessed? students, partners
- What assessment tools will be used? Observation, rubrics, product evaluation
- Who will assess? Students, partners
- How will assessment results be used? To grade students, to improve the planning process, to improve partnerships

ACCESS A FULL RANGE OF INFORMATION RESOURCES AND SERVICES. Libraries represent the most cost-effective way for a variety of children to have access to a wide range of resources to address a broad spectrum of issues. Skilled in information literacy and instruction, librarians offer an organized program of services that support the school and its work in using resources to advance learning.

Say that an art class is creating masks, and that the teacher wants students to see examples of different approaches. Alone, the teacher might find a few books in the 730s and sigh at the limited number of resources. In collaboration, the librarian can point out materials in art history and crafts, books and periodicals on world cultures, audiovisual resources (Native American videos, museum slides, events posters), digital sources (CD-ROMs on Africa, virtual mask collections, mask lessons online).

The library is no longer just a place to find a book and check it out. It's a research center where students plan their informational needs, access and assess possible sources, extract and manipulate information using a variety of methods and media, and produce a final product. For this, the library needs to provide relevant tools: viewing space, computers, camcorders and editing equipment, desktop publishing software, even magazines for collage creation. And the librarian needs to collaborate with other staff to oversee those resources and facilities.

Nor do library services stop at the library door any more. Certainly, with limited budgets and staffing, libraries cannot hope to satisfy all informational needs. But then, they never could. What the librarian possesses is the knowledge of other resources, both material and human, and the means to help the school community access them. In collaboration with local agencies, the librarian might develop a database of community resources. The librarian can work with other local libraries of all types to provide interlibrary loan or facsimile access to information. The librarian can link students to community programming opportunities at local cable companies. By providing tips on working with legislators and interest groups, the librarian can even help school lobbying efforts to improve conditions for education.

ENCOURAGE MEDIA UNDERSTANDING AND ENJOYMENT. What once was confined to reading appreciation has expanded to literacy and positive attitudes about reading, viewing, and listening. Today's students are awash in a sea of competing and cacophonic stimuli. They need opportunities to sort out all of this stuff and to reflect on it. They need to find order in the midst of it all so they can have an intellectual and psychological grasp on the subject at hand—and even enjoy the process! And they can't do it alone.

> Today's students are awash in a sea of competing and cacophonic stimuli. They need opportunities to sort out all of this stuff and to reflect on it.

A well-organized library with lots of resources in a variety of media is a first step. The librarian needs to make personal contact with the student to understand where he is coming from and what individual needs and wants are. Then the librarian can help the student find the resources that are out there waiting to be used and appreciated. Is the same information available in different formats? Does the library have viewing and listening areas? In short, do students have the *opportunity* to engage with sources that match personal needs?

Different media demand different skills for understanding and appreciation. The library might sponsor a movie club that analyzes films or display propaganda posters borrowed from a historical society with signage that explains visual manipulation. Poetry or drama read-alouds offer opportunities for students to listen critically. A guest speaker from an advertising firm can show students how marketing research has shown how people respond to mass media.

In other words, librarians must provide more than resources; they need to help students learn how to understand those resources. Partnerships facilitate this complex process.

This example shows how.

IMAGING MUSIC LESSON PLAN

ACTIVITY DESCRIPTION: Student groups create a slide-tape show of musical themes.

CONTENT OUTCOMES: Students will
- Identify musical forms.
- Identify musical themes.
- Select musical passages that exemplify a musical theme.
- Select images that portray musical themes.

INFORMATION LITERACY OUTCOMES: Students will
- Select and evaluate musical forms and themes.
- Sequence images to match musical themes.
- Transform sources into a slide-tape show.

PREREQUISITE SKILLS:
- Use reference tools to access musical and visual sources.
- Create slides from images.
- Create a slide-tape show.

MUSIC TEACHER PREPARATION:
- Teach students the concepts of musical forms and themes.
- Teach students how to evaluate musical compositions and select representative excerpts.
- Write activity guidelines.

PHOTOGRAPHY OR ART TEACHER PREPARATION:
- Teach students how to interpret artistic compositions in terms of theme or mood.
- Teach students how to create slides and slide-tape shows (as needed).

LIBRARIAN PREPARATION:
- Gather resources and, optionally, equipment.
- Bookmark relevant Web sites.
- Teach students how to access resources.
- Teach students how to tape musical excerpts (optional).

RATIONALE FOR THE PROCESS: Music often creates images in our minds. *Night on Bald Mountain, Scheherazade, Til Eulenspiegel* are all connotative or romantic pieces. Art songs, in fact, exemplify musical romanticism. Consider the choice of music that accompanies movies. This project allows students to visualize musical themes and correlate those musical images with artistic ones.

GROUP ACTIVITY:
1. Select pieces of music with similar themes or forms.
2. Select artwork that exemplifies a visual translation of the music.
3. Produce slides of the artwork.
4. Sequence the musical selections, then produce an audio cassette of the sequenced music.

5. Create a slide show by sequencing the slides to match the music order.
6. Synchronize the slides with the audiocassette.
7. Explain the rationale for the musical and artistic selection and arrangement.

TIPS: To help students understand the possible connection between music and visual images, share selections from Disney's movie *Fantasia*. Have students explain how the visual elements complement and interpret the music. Generalize the concept of "connotative" music by asking guiding questions:

- What kind of music sounds happy, sad, angry, forceful, playful?
- What kind of music makes you think of a particular place or event?
- What musical elements play into these connotations? (Key, instruments, tempo, loudness)
- What kind of art shows different emotions or different themes?
- What artistic elements create those connotations? (Color, balance, medium, space)
- How does music in movies cue one about a plot turn or character? What about MTV?

Because equipment is usually limited in schools, accomplishing this project may prove challenging. Some ways to deal with it include

- Sharing equipment through careful scheduling
- Having students bring equipment to school (possible theft problem)
- Having students do much of the work outside class.

Student groups may divide the work based on available resources (one family has a good music collection, another has a copy stand). Equity issues are very important. Schools with extended hour production labs help those students who do not have such resources at home. Note that even the cost of creating slides may be a financial constraint for some students. One alternative is to borrow a camcorder and videotape visual elements on a used tape, and then audio-insert the music using a school tape player-recorder.

Students may need parameters for creating the slide-tape show. Here is one example:

- Two to five musical passages, each lasting between 30 seconds to one minute
- Five to ten pieces of art
- Total show between two and four minutes.

Depending on the content objectives, the teacher may ask students to select only classical music or established artwork. If the concept is more expressive in nature, students might be encouraged to produce their own artwork to go with music.

ASSESSMENT:

- Groups share their slide-tape show and have peers guess the musical-artistic theme or form. Afterwards, the producers explain their process and justification of choices.
- The teacher assesses the product in terms of how well it exemplifies the theme and form, and the explanation is assessed in terms of thoroughness, basis for judgment, and group collaboration.
- The librarian assesses the group's ability to find appropriate images, and to credit them accurately.

Hopefully, schools manifest a culture of readers. Such a norm is not an accident, particularly in the face of societal values. Rather, it reflects solid collaboration on several fronts: a wide variety of reading materials to meet academic and personal needs; remedial support so all students can be successful readers; recognition of student engagement; and celebration of reading through contests, reading fests, author receptions, and participation in National Library Media Month and other events. Librarians can display great reading throughout the school; students can make reading posters for the halls; school newspapers can feature reading "testimonials"; teachers can share good books in their classrooms; school Web sites can include book chat rooms; Great Books groups can share insights; and transcripts can note exceptional reading achievements.

SUPPORT DIVERSE LEARNING.

These days the idea that one textbook could have ever been considered sufficient for all students seems silly. "One size fits all" never did apply to learning. In that respect, school libraries have always believed in a variety of materials to meet the individual needs of students. In fact, most libraries have tried to provide a variety of formats for years, knowing that different media translate information in unique ways. With mainstreaming and greater cultural diversity, education has become increasingly sensitive to students' capabilities and needs. Librarians can serve as leaders to help the rest of the school community support student diversity.

A third of California's K-12 student population has a non-English primary language. Many of their parents cannot read English. Thus, it is imperative that library materials in other languages be available to help folks make the transition to English as well as maintain their own cultures. Unfortunately, many librarians do not know the foreign languages of their clientele, so they need to work in partnership with native speakers—and expert ethnic librarians—to determine the appropriateness of the material for the library.

Even though students in special education are mainstreamed as much as possible, they still have barriers to learning. The librarian needs to work in a three-way collaboration with classroom and special education teachers to determine what learning activities are being introduced, what resources are feasible, and how to instruct students with special needs. Fortunately, most librarians have coached students individually, working from a student's area of comfort to a new plateau of knowledge. So they already possess diagnostic ability. An area of change, though, is adaptive technology. Much progress has been made in technology to meet the needs of the multiply challenged. Librarians need to know about these advances and integrate them into library services.

> These days the idea that one textbook could have ever been considered sufficient for all students seems silly. "One size fits all" never did apply to learning.

To really influence student learning so that all students can succeed, librarians need to work closely with the rest of the school community, including parents, to share resources and services. Counselors can inform librarians about particular students' needs, and librarians can suggest useful professional reading. Parents can work with librarians to teach reading comprehension. Librarians can teach parents how to use the Internet effectively and can circulate Web TV to ensure they have access to important online resources. Gifted students can coach students academically, and the library can house the tutoring service.

Special education teachers can explain ways students can get involved in their learning, and librarians can suggest materials that speak to those strengths. As librarians work with students throughout the information process, more opportunities for valuable resources and services exist.

FOSTER INQUIRY. Historically, libraries have served as lifelong centers of learning. Books were the repositories of knowledge, and libraries housed the ideas of the ages with a "come and get it" attitude. Now the emphasis is on critical evaluation of information. No word is gospel. Now, librarians need to be more involved in encouraging *engagement* with those resources. Learning can't be passive, just as libraries can't be passive. No wonder partnerships are imperative.

At its most basic level, research exemplifies the spirit of inquiry. Most librarians share an inherent enthusiasm for research. By talking through research strategies, librarians model the process for students and share their passion for learning. For that reason, many school librarians explain the research process in terms of detective work or solving a mystery. Some use a game metaphor. In any case, the idea is to appeal to the child's inner fascination with uncovering vital secrets to the universe.

Because learning occurs individually and collectively, the library should accommodate varying modes of inquiry. Ideally, the library should have small side rooms for group discussion and research engagement, carrels or other corners for distraction-free single work, computer space that can accommodate one or several people, and production space for groups and individuals to design their final projects. Likewise, librarians need to be able to instruct students in groups of different sizes and provide other teaching aids (signs, guide sheets, self-paced cassette tapes, learning stations) to meet the learning styles of different students.

Librarians need to recognize and publicize successful student inquiry results. Displaying insightful reports and presentations, posting student reviews of good books, adding in-depth hypermedia files to a common library online archive—all are ways to model the possibilities of student investigations. Particularly if librarians help assess student work, they see the fruits of student—and librarian—labor and can determine which products best demonstrate information competency.

INTEGRATE TECHNOLOGY. At this point, school librarians cannot afford to be out of the technology loop. Let's face it, some graduate library schools have even dropped the term "library," replacing it with the term "information science/studies." Obviously, information and ideas come in all forms, and organization of that information involves technology. Technology is actually a logical part of librarianship because of its storage and retrieval aspects, but some librarians still feel uncomfortable with it. However, even that feeling can be productive if it leads the librarian to confront the concern and learn how to use technology to better serve the school. In that way, he'll let other reluctant souls know that they, too, can learn. If the librarian collaborates in the process, learning from some and teaching others, the probability increases that technology will be integrated throughout the school.

Technology can be expensive. And it's not always needed. The library is the most cost-effective way to provide access to technology and its resources in an organized fashion. The

> ...Many school librarians explain the research process in terms of detective work or solving a mystery. Some use a game metaphor.

library is open throughout the day and accessible to all. Staff know how to make good educational use of the technology and supervise it carefully to maintain it in good condition. Why buy several cameras to use occasionally when one or two can be circulated from the library? Library aides can be taught how to videotape and edit, freeing the classroom teacher to use the medium to enhance learning in the classroom.

Of course, such accessibility comes at a price: the cost of sharing. Teachers have to work with the librarian and other teachers to schedule equipment and staff use. But in these times of budget constraints (Did any school ever have more than enough funds?) resource sharing is necessary, and the library provides a well-established, successful model for it.

One of the strengths of the library media program is identifying what strategies and resources are most effective to answer an informational need. It's probably faster to find a picture of a state flag in an encyclopedia, get currency rates in a newspaper, or locate a copy of the Bill of Rights in an almanac than on the Internet. On the other hand, finding treatments of rare diseases, the weather now in Cambodia, or business information can be a network away. Want to capture movement? Use a camcorder. Want visual documentation? Use a camera. Want to encourage interactive learning? Use hypermedia.

Librarians can work with teachers and students to develop a wide repertoire of technological tools that fit each inquiry. Librarians can also model the use of technology in their own instruction, such as the use of screen "dumps" transparencies to show how to use the online catalog or bookmarking Web-based tutorials on evaluating Internet sources.

> One of the strengths of the library media program is identifying what strategies and resources are most effective to answer an informational need.

Educational technology has expanded access to information and means to process it. The question is how do students learn and apply those skills? Before, the world of information was a relatively closed universe within school walls, defined by textbook adoption procedures and librarian selection policies. Now students *must* learn how to evaluate information critically and shape it according to the problem or need at hand. Whose job is it to teach students? When are those skills incorporated into assignments?

One approach to this challenge is to establish a technology committee composed of subject or grade level representatives along with the librarian and technology specialist (if one is available). As a group, the tech committee determines what technological skills students should demonstrate, who will teach those skills, at what level and standard, and what opportunities students will have to practice those skills. Often, for such learning to take place, teachers themselves have to learn those technological skills and figure out how to integrate them meaningfully into the curriculum. As a team, the tech committee can teach its members those educational techniques as well as train its own constituents.

LINK WITH THE LARGER COMMUNITY. Today's library is the informational doorway to the world, reflecting the global nature of learning. Just as education now emphasizes the application of school learning experiences to the "real world," so the library should model lifelong learning that connects with the world. This is the ultimate partnership.

The library can serve as an orderly microcosm of the world, a safe space where students can explore their surroundings and investigate possibilities. Particularly with the advent of the Internet, librarians can help students discern the true from the untrue, to develop and apply criteria for evaluation and decision-making. Students cannot be protected from the world; rather, they need to know how to cope in the world and not be controlled by it. Information literacy is the key.

Librarians can help the school community connect with the larger community, giving access to local and regional resources. Library Web pages can be a link to community sources. Library aides can work in the public library or other government agencies. Local groups can sponsor programs and information sessions that the library can publicize or co-host. Librarians can help students identify internship and volunteer opportunities in the community. Librarians can speak with parent groups about lifelong literacy. They can help the school gain access to public programming channels to broadcast educational events.

Probably the most effective link to the larger community is through school personnel, particularly classroom teachers. When librarians collaborate with teachers, they indirectly influence every student and parent. Helping teachers see the opportunities in the larger community, and encouraging those partnerships, offers visible proof that education is a lifelong societal endeavor. By having good relationships in the community, librarians can suggest valuable speakers, promote youth vote programs, and get local industry to offer job shadowing opportunities for both students and teachers. They can spearhead technology fairs. They can find grant opportunities. The universe of learning and partnerships is limited only by one's imagination.

> **INFORMATION ACCESS AND DELIVERY**

The mission of the library media program is to provide physical and intellectual access to materials in all forms. Without resources, students have nothing to grapple with, to learn from. On another level, libraries bring together great ideas. It is only as strong as the availability of those great thoughts for young minds: ideas that are accurate, current, and relevant. In these days of resource sharing, this task demands strong, effective partnerships.

PROVIDE INTELLECTUAL ACCESS TO INFORMATION AND IDEAS. Librarians are idea people who want to share those ideas with others. The best material in the world can be in the library, but if students can't understand it, then it isn't useful. While some sources may be beyond the intellectual grasp of a student, say a Spanish short story anthology for a non-Spanish reader, most materials can be understood with a little guidance. Librarians must work collaboratively with classroom teachers and other school personnel to help students become information competent.

Librarians normally don't "translate" obscure references or do the students' reading for them; rather, they teach *processes* that enable students to ferret out the information for themselves and interpret it fairly. Some of those skills include using tables of contents and indexes to locate facts, determining point of view, distinguishing between fact and opinion, analyzing graphic and numeric information, verifying data, finding patterns and trends, testing hypotheses. These techniques are most effectively learned when woven into classroom

> When librarians collaborate with teachers, they indirectly influence every student and parent.

assignments. When librarians plan assignments with teachers from the start, these skills can be introduced in an orderly manner. Likewise, if librarians help assess student process and product, they can modify instruction to improve student success rates.

A significant aspect of intellectual access is research strategy: a plan for locating and selecting information. Librarians can work with teachers to provide bibliographies, "pathways," Internet site bookmarks, and WebQuests that help students use keywords and other means to find the information they want.

On a systemic basis, librarians can work with other departments or teacher groups to ensure that students learn how to access information intellectually. Essentially, the school staff needs to ascertain how students access information intellectually now, determine what intellectual gaps exist, and fill those gaps. The exciting part of this process is the interaction among teachers and librarians as they determine the most effective way to help students understand information. The goal is to develop a system whereby teachers can rely on each other and the librarian to help students develop the skills needed to use information in a meaningful manner.

E-mail constitutes one way for students to gain knowledge about research methods, as the following example demonstrates:

PROVIDE PHYSICAL ACCESS TO RESOURCES. One aspect of librarianship is physical access to sources. These days, that physical access can be virtual as libraries hook up to cyberlibraries and other repositories of information. At the other end of the access spectrum, the library needs to ensure that all students can get to the material they need by making sure shelving isn't too high or keywords aren't too difficult to manage. Partnerships arise as librarians work with their constituencies to provide thorough access.

Students can feel lost in the library. They need clear signage, user-friendly subject headings, and an organized way to find the materials they need. Librarians should work with their clientele to find out where glitches in locating information occur and determine ways to help those people to use the library independently.

Does the library offer an organized and easy-to-use way to locate needed materials? Has the librarian worked with ESL teachers to provide signage in appropriate languages? Perhaps a user-friendly sub-collection is needed to help students transition to the major collection.

Does the librarian work with special education teachers to provide adaptive technology and other means to ensure equitable access to needed sources? Computer peripherals may need to be modified, and display options may need adjusting because the working surface itself needs to accommodate students with special needs. Books on tape may need to be made available for sight-limited students. Usually, the librarian needs to work with relevant teachers to ensure that those students get the resources they need.

PROVIDE A CLIMATE FOR LEARNING. Librarians want the library to be a safe and quiet haven for students to read and research. They have a duty to provide comfortable seating and a variety of settings to accommodate different styles of learning, but the entire school community sets the atmosphere in the library for learning. How many times have librarians had to approach other staff about sitting on the tables, drinking, talking loudly, and otherwise distracting other students from their involvement with resources? Climate-building is not a job to be accomplished in isolation; it needs effective collaboration.

When students walk into the library, do they feel welcome? What subliminary messages are communicated? In an elementary

ONLINE HOMEWORK HELP CHECKLIST

Follow these steps to ensure online homework success.

1. **Get organized.** Getting homework done fast and correctly takes organization, whether or not you use the Internet. Do your homework at the same time every night, gather all necessary materials together, and turn off the TV.
2. **Read the assignment.** Be sure you understand what is required of you and what subject areas the homework covers.
3. **Available time?** If it's easier and faster to use a book or magazine to complete your work, use them! Don't spend time searching for information on the Net if you can find it faster somewhere else.
4. **Which Internet resources?** First, ask yourself if the Internet is the best tool for your assignment. If you're writing a paper, the Internet can deliver sources to make your work better. But if your teacher asks you to define words scattered throughout a textbook chapter you're reading for next Monday's class, using the Internet isn't the best way to complete the assignment.
   - Next, think about which Internet resources will help you most. You can use these tools in all kinds of ways for all sorts of homework assignments. Here are a few things you can do.
   - Communicate with people one-to-one. You may be able to use e-mail to complete all assignments by communicating with peers, experts, and many others: **http://www.keypals.com**
   - Track down up-to-date information. The Internet is full of up-to-the-minute news reports from newspapers worldwide, thousands of up-to-date databases, and even hourly satellite images taken from every corner of the globe: **http://www.cnn.com** and **http://www.intellicast.com**
   - Information gathering from experts and others. Say you have to interview a famous local person for an assignment. Why focus on your local area when you could interview an astronaut in space or an award-winning author via e-mail: **http://www.askanexpert.com**
5. **Internet search tools.** Determine which Internet directories and search engines can best help you find the information you need. Then, decide which "keywords" will give you the best search results: **http://www.connectedteacher.com/tips/tips.asp**
6. **Search strategy.** Once you've got your keywords, decide how much time and how many search engines you want to use. You should run your keywords through at least three search tools such as *HotBot*, *Alta Vista*, and *MetaCrawler*.
7. **Go online.** Fire up your modem and get started! Stay focused while online. Use a timer if necessary. An hour searching is enough time to discover whether the Internet will help.
8. **Critically judge the information you find.** Take a critical look at it to determine whether the information is authentic and valid. Anything can be published to a worldwide audience in seconds via the Net. This "information" could read like something from your textbook. But it could contain inaccurate, unsubstantiated, or misleading facts.
9. **Cite the Internet information you use.** Be sure to cite the online sources in your bibliography. You'll find information on citing these sources at **http://www.classroom.com/resource/citingnetresources.asp**

library, if there are no inviting pictures or student-related features in the library, then youngsters will not feel comfortable. Imagine a library where tables and chairs do not accommodate smaller bodies or reading areas do not allow students to relax. If librarians do not transmit a message of hospitality and acceptance, students will not feel comfortable. They will be less likely to ask the librarian for help, and they will probably be less successful in accessing the information they need. Librarians need to collaborate with students to find out what aspects of the library would make them feel more accepted.

Shared expectations are a key to climate control. As the librarian works with the classroom teacher to design learning experiences, he needs to talk about behavior in the library. What factors promote learning? A balance between silence and chaos needs to be negotiated to ensure a climate where students can feel comfortable working together but are not distracted by other students. If the librarian and teacher agree on a level of sound and range of acceptable behaviors and communicate them with the students, a healthier atmosphere will result.

The tone of the library extends beyond students and faculty to include parents and the larger community. When the librarian welcomes parent volunteers and gives them meaningful tasks to perform, those community members feel they are contributing to the library's mission and they communicate that atmosphere to other parents. When community members are invited to speak at the school library or donate materials to the library, they transmit that inclusion to other community members who reinforce the library's learning climate. For instance, the library might hold a town meeting on a social issue or sponsor a community-wide book discussion group. Both activities demonstrate the library's effort to involve local people to take advantage of the library as a learning environment and to reinforce learning for the school's chief clientele—students.

PROVIDE EQUITABLE ACCESS. Students need to learn when they need to learn. Simple. The library cannot operate on a rigid 50-minutes-every-other-Tuesday schedule. Because learning is so organic and needs-based, collaboration among teachers and librarians is essential.

Flexible scheduling is a key to optimal learning. As librarians and teachers work together to design learning activities, they have to determine where learning will occur and when. With the advent of technology and computer labs, even more coordination is needed to assure technology access as well as other means to manipulate information. And space is not enough. Students and teachers need experts to help them navigate through the information and cull the important aspects. So technology specialists as well as librarians and classroom teachers have to determine ahead of time what skills need to be available to students and what training students need to be independent information processors.

The following guidelines provide insight into scheduling issues for in-depth projects:

> **Shared expectations are a key to climate control.**

A MODEL TIME FRAME FOR CLASS LIBRARY RESEARCH PROJECTS

PLANNING:
- Teacher talks with librarian about assignment and schedules class or resources.
- Other prep activities may include librarian-generated bibliography or Web bookmarks, reserve shelf.
- Determine what role librarian will play: instructor, trainer of student experts, individual coach.
- Determine what part of the library or what services students will use: computers, reference room, magazine area, production area.

THE DAY BEFORE:
- Teacher explains assignment with students in classroom.
- Teacher and students brainstorm possible questions, sources (periodicals, regular books, CD-ROM, videos, references, telecommunications), and strategies.
- Assign members for small groups, determine group roles.
- Students identify what they don't know how to find or use (magazine indexes, Internet).
- Teacher contacts librarian about concerns.
- For machine use (for instance, how to use a CD-ROM product), have several students go to the library during group discussion to be trained on needed equipment.
- If librarian provides teacher a bibliography or other handout, photocopy and distribute it.

FIRST DAY:
- Clarify any last-minute issues and take class to library as a group.
- Librarian gives any needed instruction or guidelines based on planning and student list of needs.
- Reiterate instructions on machine use, as appropriate.
- Students go for it! Librarian helps as needed.
- The last five minutes, assemble students and have them process their search strategies, successes, and needs with teacher and librarian.

SECOND DAY:
- Students go to library and continue their work. Librarian helps and intervenes as needed.
- The list five minutes, have students process their research session.

THIRD DAY:
- Students work with available information in the classroom or lab.
- Teacher discusses student findings to this point. Students may have peaked at this point and know what other materials they need. Perhaps they have finished the first portion of their research and need to process to the next research strategy step.
- Those students needing more time to research come to the library, preferably one or two at a time, to access needed information.
- As teacher sees the need, he contacts the librarian to schedule another period in the library.
- New needs and resources can be brought to the librarian's attention.

FOURTH DAY (OPTIONAL):
- Students go the library as a whole, with the librarian instructing and coaching as needed.
- The last five minutes, have students process their research session.

Students with unusual needs may require "extra" attention. In reality, they are just trying to get the same access as others but have more challenges or barriers to deal with. Thus, visually impaired and dyslexic students may need audiobooks. Non-English-speaking students need materials in their own language so they can understand concepts. A wide variety of materials in different formats should be available to address the different capabilities and needs of diverse students. Even equipment and furniture may be adjusted to accommodate the physical needs of students (lower shelving and desks, distraction-free carrels, special computer peripherals). Librarians need to collaborate with educators who work closely with these students to acquire and use the right kinds of resources.

Students need access to information beyond the library walls and daily schedule, so the librarian needs to collaborate with others to provide such access. Print and non-print materials can be loaned for classroom use. CD-ROMs and databases can be networked for access from any linked computer station throughout the school. Videos can be broadcast if the school has the requisite cabled system; otherwise, videos can be borrowed to be played in another room. Particularly if the library has a Web page with Web-based catalog and access to online databases, the entire community can access information from home. And for those students who can't afford computers at home, devices such as Web TV can be circulated so all students can have access to Internet and library resources.

DEVELOP AND EVALUATE COLLECTIONS COLLABORATIVELY. Since the library's collection supports the school's mission, it makes sense for that collection to be the result of collaboration. It would be hard to imagine a librarian selecting materials without any reference to the school's curriculum and population. Yet an active partnership is called for beyond general observation and passive interaction. And it makes sense, for even if the best and most appropriate materials are put on the shelves, if no one knows about them or had any part in their selection, those materials will sit on the shelves. Furthermore, if the library doesn't have the resources expected by others, then its credibility suffers as much as the collection.

What are the users' needs and wants? That's the key question. The entire school needs to answer it: students, faculty, support staff, administration, parents, and community members who use the library. It should be noted that needs may differ from wants. People may *want* an original Gutenberg Bible, but may only *need* several current versions of the Bible in English. Sometimes users don't know their own because they haven't had enough experience with resources. And until the community participates, the librarian really doesn't know all of their wants or needs.

Others may know about welcome additions to the collection that the librarian doesn't know about, such as professional reading or agency videotapes. All must be involved to get the full picture. This task must be done in the context of the school's curriculum, co-curricular activities, and their delivery. However, the school's workings should be interpreted broadly; counselors may need diagnostic information, maintenance may require technical manuals, peer tutors may want coaching techniques. So the librarian should observe classes and other

> **Students with unusual needs may require "extra" attention. In reality, they are just trying to get the same access as others but have more challenges or barriers to deal with.**

activities to see what kind of resources align best with existing or desired practice.

Collection development also has to complement the existing collection. This task involves examining the present collection in light of identified needs, noting gaps or materials that need to be withdrawn, and acquiring materials that can be integrated into the collection. Once materials are acquired and put on the shelf, they are immediately evaluated by the school community who determine whether the available items satisfy their needs. Library partners may also use formal criteria to assess the present collection and suggest ways to expand and complement it.

Interestingly, while most teachers feel comfortable with selection policies and the librarian's choices of books, they might not think that the librarian is competent to evaluate software and other digital materials. "Who has that breadth and depth of knowledge and experience?" they may ask. While the librarian could point out personal competence, it's more effective to collaborate with others in locating and using reviewing sources and other selection tools. That way, several partners have access to specific evaluation sources: organizational lists, academic coursework, discipline-based Internet sites. The underlying issues in accepting other people's evaluations are credible criteria for assessment and authority of the reviewer. Librarians can also have others preview and evaluate materials; this practice empowers the reviewer and helps ensure that he knows about the resource and shares it with others.

PROMOTE INTELLECTUAL FREEDOM. School libraries probably have more challenges about their collections than other types of libraries, partly because of the age of the students, partly because of local control, and partly because of the particular curriculum or mission of the school. Religious schools, for instance, may not want the library to collect materials counter to their beliefs. Since the library should support the curriculum, some schools may take exception to information about skateboarding or body piercing. Internet access frightens a number of people, who may want to force the library to add filters to the network. It's easy enough to hide under the cover of limited budgets, but with access to the Internet, it's no longer as easy to shy away from intellectual freedom issues. Particularly if the library is challenged for its stance, partners are vital to the library's principles.

> It's easy enough to hide under the cover of limited budgets, but with access to the Internet, it's no longer as easy to shy away from intellectual freedom issues.

School libraries need collection policies. Sometimes these decisions rest with state codes or local governing bodies. Sometimes librarians can craft them, although procedures are more likely to be the librarian's province.

Where possible, other school members should be part of the policy-making process. Administrators are particularly useful because they usually have legal information that could influence library practice, such as grievance policies. On the other hand, existing documents such as the *Library Bill of Rights* and other intellectual freedom statements may be unknown to the rest of the school community and should be shared with them.

Libraries can work with community groups to host events that support the concept of intellectual freedom: student voting during local and national elections, town meetings about local controversies, Banned Book Week, panelists on human rights issues.

The most natural way, though, to foster intellectual freedom is to partner with teachers in developing thought-provoking learning activities. Have students debate issues, create pro-con posters on topics, create simulations where each student assumes a different role or viewpoint on a controversial issue. The librarian needs to make sure that resources are available to support multiple interpretations. In that respect, the Internet is especially valuable because so many different views are articulated about all kinds of subjects. As librarians and classroom teachers work together, helping students probe behind stances to discover underlying assumptions and look for supporting evidence, they foster a lifelong habit of open inquiry and independent decision-making.

REFLECT LEGAL AND PROFESSIONAL PRACTICE. Information is not value-neutral. Youngsters have to deal with complex issues, and the options can be threatening to the community and society in general. So while libraries may seem like safe havens of civilization, they are actually hotbeds of potential revolution—certainly of independent thought. The issue is not so much what subject is being treated, but how it is being treated. As part of the educational system, the library has the obligation to show students how to deal with information responsibly. Particularly since ethical and legal behavior is societally driven, librarians need to model and teach these principles in collaboration with school personnel and the community. As a representative of both education and librarianship, the librarian has a double duty in this matter—and twice the number of possible partners.

What is legal? The library needs to make resources about legalities accessible to all. Of particular importance are materials on juvenile rights, laws affecting students with special needs, educational codes, copyright laws, and community regulations. Most of these materials are specialized and some are hard to locate, so librarians need to work with local governmental agencies to provide them. In some cases, Internet access and facsimile services offer realistic means to attain needed information.

Librarians need to know what legalities and professional ethics affect the school library media program. Librarians need to maintain close contact with their professional organizations, such as the American Library Association and teacher organizations, to keep current on legal and ethical developments. They also need to mirror those stances in everyday operations: ensuring universal access to online sources, maintaining confidentiality of circulation records, staying in compliance with copyright laws.

> So while libraries may seem like safe havens of civilization, they are actually hotbeds of potential revolution—certainly of independent thought.

Librarians need to play a part in legal and ethical issues that arise in the school. In curriculum development, librarians can point out the importance of programs that address the needs of a variety of students. They can work with special education teachers to make sure their students have the resources they need and are entitled to under the law. They can provide materials that will help student government operate ethically. They can help parents learn what their legal rights are in educating their children. In all cases, librarians can model ethical behavior, and act as professional exemplars of ethical decision-making.

▶ PROGRAM ADMINISTRATION

Librarians do not have free reign in the library, although some people might think so. Indeed, the library media program must be aligned with the school's mission, and the school's partnership must be visible as it supports library staffing, funding, and management. As any librarian knows, when the library operates independently or at odds with the rest of the school, the program will be ineffective at best and probably dysfunctional. On the other hand, when the entire school promotes itself and works in tandem with the library staff to offer effective services, then a true learning community can blossom.

SUPPORT THE SCHOOL. It makes sense to support the school since its mission is student learning. There's a real sense of "we're all in this together for the sake of the kids." However, it's all too easy for the librarian to stay within the four walls of the library and act almost autonomously. If librarians want others to join them, then they need to extend their own hands and hearts outside their safe little universe.

Because the library usually has more space and display areas than most other rooms in the school, it can easily exhibit student work, post articles about the school, and hold special events or speaking engagements. It can publicize school activities on bulletin boards and Web pages, promote celebrations through book tie-ins and library newsletters, and provide background information for coming events.

As the school develops policies and standards for learning, the librarian needs to make sure that the library presence is highly visible. Librarians need to sit on decision-making boards. Technology should be integrated across the curriculum. Matriculation requirements should include demonstrating information competence.

Where does the library fit in? Particularly when schools study themselves or undergo reform, librarians need to articulate their programs and support their efforts. For example, the Western Association of Schools and Colleges (WASC) is the accreditation board for Pacific states institutions. In their *Focusing on Learning* document, WASC categorizes school effort into five domains: vision and culture, powerful teaching and learning, curricular paths, student support, and assessment. The library ought to see itself in each domain and show how it works with the rest of the school to achieve success.

If the library keeps a copy of research assignments and resultant student work, it can provide these documents as evidence of student effort. If the library provides videotaping or editing service, student aides can tape the school in action and edit the tape for the visiting team to examine.

PLAN STRATEGICALLY. Vision without a plan is a dream. While most librarians can plan great libraries, collaboration is needed to make sure that those plans are in synch with the rest of the school and accepted by the community. Particularly when school demographics shift and present practice is called into question, the librarian needs to keep abreast of changes so the library program plan can remain viable. True, coordination of effort, even in the planning stages, takes time and demands shared control, but the results will be more meaningful and the activities are more likely to be supported and carried out.

Student information literacy standards are a simple and effective way to begin planning. In concert with other teachers, the librarian can map out existing assignments that address those standards and determine what instruction is now given for students to

> There's a real sense of "we're all in this together for the sake of the kids." However, it's all too easy for the librarian to stay within the four walls of the library and act almost autonomously

learn those skills. By identifying gaps in incorporating these standards, the librarian can be instrumental in modifying curriculum and strengthening the library program.

For content areas, librarians can work with curriculum experts to ensure that appropriate resources are available. Particularly when new courses are developed, the librarian needs to participate in the planning so collection development can reflect the change.

Many schools now recognize the existing and potential impact of technology on learning. If the librarian does not participate in these discussions, the library may turn into a museum and the librarian be replaced by a technology specialist. If the librarian is behind technologically, then he needs to work with technology experts to get up to speed. If the librarian is ahead technologically (relatively speaking), then he needs to share expertise and help direct the future of its incorporation into the curriculum, as well as ensure that the library provides the resources and level of service needed for students to take advantage of emerging technologies.

DO ONGOING ASSESSMENT. Every plan needs to be evaluated, even if it is never carried out. And every action needs to be evaluated to determine whether to continue in the same direction or change. Typically, assessment is done by at least two people or groups (preferably three) using at least two different instruments. In this way, triangulation of results can verify the data and provide a sound basis for decision-making. Obviously, then, assessment of the library media program needs to involve partners. No matter the outcome, the library benefits:

Students and teachers can assess specific class visits using comment cards such as one finds in airlines and restaurants.

Librarians should provide regular opportunities for feedback: ongoing suggestion boxes, notebooks, or Web-based response sheets; collection reviewing and weeding sessions; evaluations of events and programs; and focus group discussions on library service.

A simple library use survey form follows:

Using *Information Power's* program principles, librarians can survey the school to find out how others rate the relative importance of each principle. They can also find out whom the rest of the school perceives as the person or group with the most power to influence conforming to each principle. These data can help the librarian determine which partnerships might be the most effective. For instance, if there is general agreement that the principal is the most influential in promoting collaborative planning, then the librarian needs to work closely with him to make that happen. If the school community agrees that a climate conducive to learning is important, then the librarian needs to put extra effort into that area. (This approach is the current research focus of the author. Please contact her if interested in participating in this project.)

DO ONGOING STAFF DEVELOPMENT. School librarianship has changed drastically over the years, particularly with the incorporation of technology. As educators, librarians not only need to keep current about library science for themselves, but they can be professional

	OTHERS THINK PROGRAM IS GOOD	OTHERS THINK PROGRAM IS BAD
Librarian thinks program is good	Celebrate! Plan for even better	Educate others
Librarian thinks program is bad	Raise expectations; improve	Plan together for improvement

HIGH SCHOOL USE SURVEY FOR STUDENTS

By completing this survey of your library, you can help us improve library service.

1. How often do you use the library? (Circle one)

    Daily   Weekly   Monthly   Quarterly

2. Which of the following kinds of resources do you use in the library? (Circle as many as apply)

    Books   Magazines   Newspapers   Photocopier

    Reference books   CD-ROMs   Clippings and pamphlets   Scanner

    Indexes (*Reader's Guide, Infotrac, MAS*)   Microfiche

    Word-processing computers   Book lists   Sales books

3. The librarian creates an attractive learning environment.

    Strongly agree   Somewhat agree   Somewhat disagree   Strongly disagree

4. The librarian is knowledgeable about library services.

    Strongly agree   Somewhat agree   Somewhat disagree   Strongly disagree

5. The librarian is helpful in making suggestions about sources that might be useful.

    Strongly agree   Somewhat agree   Somewhat disagree   Strongly disagree

6. The librarian is helpful in assisting you with your library work when you ask for help.

    Strongly agree   Somewhat agree   Somewhat disagree   Strongly disagree

7. How would you rate the library's collection?

    Great   Usually good   Adequate   Inadequate

If you wish to expand on the answers above, or make additional comments about the library, please use the space below:

growth mentors as well. Let's face it. Getting too far ahead of the pack can be lonely—and no one will take advantage of what's being offered. It's more rewarding for the entire school community to learn together.

Librarians can share continuing education experiences with colleagues through in-service training, newsletters, e-mail, and readings. When others attend conferences and professional growth events, librarians can ask to be included in the debriefing or offer Web space for the participant to share new insights.

Librarians can serve as mentors for teachers, either formally or through social contact. They can provide SDI (selective dissemination of information) services to staff, matching individual interests with information that comes across the library threshold. They can serve on staff development committees, helping to design workshops that address current educational needs. They can provide background information and research, and can identify experts who are available to train staff either in person or through distance learning.

A workshop framework and sample in-service session follows:

WORKSHOP FRAMEWORK

TITLE OF WORKSHOP State the major focus of the session.

INTENDED AUDIENCE Identify the most appropriate grade level or subject area.

OBJECTIVES What audience should accomplish as a result of the workshop.

SETUP Include everything the trainer needs to know to plan, organize, and conduct the workshop: group format, equipment and supply needs, additional help.

WORKSHOP OVERVIEW Summarize the sequence of activities: What will happen and how long will it take?

CONTENT:
Early bird activity
Introduction
Rationale for skill
Sample skill activities
Resources
Applications
Wrap-up
Go into detail on each area above. Include the trainer's instructions to the audience, at least in outline form. Note the strategies and resources to be used for each part of the workshop.

RESOURCES Handouts, bibliographies, and other learning aids.

ASSESSMENT How will the trainer check for understanding and determine whether learners will be able to apply their skills independently? Provide for participants to evaluate the workshop, and include follow-up assessment.

EVALUATION FORM

WORKSHOP TITLE: _____ **Date:** _____

Rate the following aspects of this workshop in terms of presentation quality, your interest, and applicability (4–excellent, 3–good, 2–adequate, 1–needs improvement).

TOPIC	QUALITY	INTEREST	USE
Sample activities	4 3 2 1	4 3 2 1	4 3 2 1
Resources	4 3 2 1	4 3 2 1	4 3 2 1
Arrangements	4 3 2 1	4 3 2 1	4 3 2 1

Complete the following:

One part of the workshop that I especially liked was:

One activity I plan to do as a result of this workshop is:

SAMPLE WORKSHOP: Teaching Teachers for Technology

During this workshop we will
- Examine characteristics of adult learners
- Plan a workshop
- Look at training methods
- Discuss creating training aids
- Detail workshop presentations

Who are adult learners?
- Self-directed
- Experienced
- Realistic
- Want applications
- Interactive
- Need repetition
- Have limited time

Obstacles to adult learning
- Fear of criticism
- Negative past training
- Competing priorities
- Bad pacing
- Not in control
- Lack of time

Experiential learning cycle
- Experience
- Examine
- Explain
- Generalize
- Apply

Implications for technology
- Make it useful
- Make it hands-on
- Let people share
- Deal with mixed abilities
- Consider variety of learning styles
- Be prepared
- Be supportive

Planning training: overall
- Outcomes
- Audience
- Format
- Time frame
- Facilities
- Resources
- Administration
- Evaluation

Planning outcomes
- Who is the audience?
- What will they be able to do?
- Under what conditions?
- To what degree?
- How will the training be applied?

Planning for the audience
- Who is the audience?
- What do they already know?
- What should they know by the end?
- What barriers exist?
- What learning styles need to be addressed?

Commercial: People remember . . .
- Five percent of what they hear.
- Ten percent of what they read.
- Twenty percent of what they read *and* hear.
- Thirty percent of what they see.
- Fifty percent of what they see *and* hear.
- Seventy percent of what they say and write.
- Ninety percent of what they do.
- Ninety-five percent of what they teach.

Planning format
- Classroom presentation
- Manuals
- Job aids
- Computer-based training
- Videotape
- Online
- Distance learning

Planning time frame
- Number of sessions
- Length of sessions
- Pacing
- Follow-up

Planning facilities
- Space
- Room arrangement
- Equipment
- Electricity
- Communications tools
- Supplies
- Food
- Human needs

Planning resources
- Human: Who will teach?
- Training aids
- Reference tools
- Handouts
- Recording devices
- Base on the task and the learner

Planning administration
- Needs assessment
- Publicity
- Registration
- Setup
- Funding
- Printing
- Catering
- Evaluation

Planning evaluation
- Outcomes-based
- What is evaluated?
- Who evaluates?
- How is evaluation done?
- When is evaluation done?
- So what?

Training methods
- Presentation
- Question-and-answer
- Small group discussion
- Demonstration and practice
- Case study and simulation

Presentation
- Communicate main ideas in a short time
- Have a strong opening and closing
- Use visual aids
- Include other training techniques
- Burden is on the trainer.

Question-and-answer
- Know your topic
- Know the type of questions to ask
- Watch the time
- Stimulate thinking
- Good for uninformed audiences
- Involve the learner

Small group discussion
- Give clear direction
- Listen attentively
- Group heterogeneously
- Circulate among groups
- Guide, don't influence
- Report out

Demonstration and practice
- Do demo yourself
- Keep demo simple
- Make sure all can see and hear
- Let learners practice
- Group in twos and threes
- Keep learners involved
- Give immediate feedback

Case study or simulation
- Focus on problem analysis
- Encourage questions
- Encourage different solutions
- Relate topic to real life
- Requires much development time

Buddy coaching
- Time intensive
- Good for specific and need-to-know basis
- Use for guide sheet development
- Encourage partnership

Conducting workshops
- Sequencing and pacing
- Training aids
- Group structure
- Assessment
- Tips

Sequencing and pacing
- Early bird
- Introduction
- Warm-up
- Activity
- Practice and application
- Resources
- Closing

Training aids
- Transparencies
- Charts
- Displays
- Videotapes
- Slides and tapes
- Computer multimedia
- Games and simulations

Group structures
- Task groups
- Discussion groups
- Brainstorming groups
- Tutorial groups
- Explorer groups

Assessment factors
- Content: difficulty, theory into practice, useful
- Delivery: format, pace, sequence, clarity
- Time: date, time of day, workshop length
- Space: size, arrangement, seating, condition
- Resources: handouts, aids, equipment
- Do at workshop and follow up

Presentation tips
- Be organized
- Define terms and give examples
- Highlight critical elements
- Use concrete words, active verbs
- *Do* things
- Check for understanding
- Be prepared

Tips to involve learners
- Give handouts with blanks to fill in
- Include breakout groups for discussion
- Use games, simulations, or role play
- Include hands-on practice
- Incorporate projects
- Have question cards or sheets
- Keep pace up
- Have fun!

COMMUNICATE CLEARLY. In the final analysis, the best library media program in the world won't benefit anyone if no one knows about it or understands it. (And it probably won't be much good if it did not include collaboration.) Partners help make the program work because they are involved from the start, help shape and assess it, and use it. And they can act as the library's best advocates, sharing the good news about it.

Librarians need to keep good records of library plans, achievements, and assessments. They can share those documents with the entire school community through publications, telecommunications, and presentations.

Librarians can point out how the library program supports other school efforts through Web pages, displays, videotapes, and assessment of student work.

Librarians can keep track of research about the impact of the school library media programs on student achievement and share those findings with the entire school. Library plans can incorporate the research to strengthen existing programs.

CHAPTER 7

The Partnership Community and Lifelong Learning

Today is the day you make your choices for tomorrow.
It takes courage to push yourself to places that you have never
been before, to test your limits, to break through barriers.

The library media program can never be the same once partnerships become a way of life. Thank goodness! As a variety of constituents interact with the library, help shape it, and integrate it into their own practice, the library becomes metaphorically the woof in the school's fabric. The learning community would unravel without it, and the library would be useless if it pulled away from that weave. Because of partnerships schools should look different. Students should look different. Learning should look different. And all should be improved.

▶ CHANGING ROLES

A culture of partnerships changes the school's educational norms and creates a new climate for learning. If the business world's Theory X describes a traditional hierarchical school, and Theory Y describes a school with participatory management, then Theory Z describes the school where the community is organized into near autonomous "houses" composed of teachers, administrators, support staff, and students. In none of those theories, though, does the role of the librarian change much; he serves either as a consultant or support person.

Instead, current thinking about organizations posits a flatter, more organic, ad hoc knowledge network rather than formal bureaucratic structure. The power shift is horizontal as all players have a say. Instead of one boss, there are several supervisors, and any of them may be challenged. People organize according to need and evolve as the situation dictates. Emphasis is on empowering rather than overpowering others. The challenge in such a fluid system is stability; the advantage is flexibility. The means to attain the end can shift in quick response to needs.

How does that play out in the school environment? The learning community is an equal opportunity employer; each person is a potential partner. Collaboration may last one hour or a lifetime, depending on the goal. Likewise, the number of people involved in a collaborative effort can range from two to everyone—and change throughout the process. People may be involved simultaneously in several partnerships, each one unique and fulfilling a part of the school's vision. The "glue" that keeps the school focused is a system of planning, communication, and assessment based on common goals.

This vision has heavy implications for the librarian's role. On top of management and instructional skills, today's librarians have to incorporate technology and expand assessment competencies. They also need to draw upon adult education skills as they increasingly coach and plan with peers. In the past, the librarian was sometimes viewed as a handmaiden to the school; now the librarian needs to be seen as a proactive educational leader. Such a transformation takes courage as well as skill.

> **In the past, the librarian was sometimes viewed as a handmaiden to the school; now the librarian needs to be seen as a proactive educational leader.**

▶ CHANGING INFORMATION

At the same time that there's an information glut, there's an information dearth. The question isn't finding information, it's accessing *good* information and using it. Each person in the school community has access to valuable information. Some people hoard information because information is power. Partners do just the opposite: share information and power freely. The interesting result is that all those who participate in that sharing gain both information and power. Moreover, the more that partners know about each other, the better they can filter out less useful information and pass on the real nuggets.

Information itself changes form with the advent of partnerships. Not only is content shared, such as good subject knowledge, but also information about *process*, such as successful lesson plans and ways to explain concepts. We've gone from "what" to "how" and "why." Because partners communicate regularly, information sharing becomes timely and informal—to borrow a business concept, "just in time." So there's more e-mail use, quick notes, voice mail updates, hallway conversations, snippets as needed. Knowing that there's a culture of collaboration, people will be more inclined to pass along material. The librarian may cringe as a good "find" is borrowed from the library and read by seven people before it returns. But if the seven people read the material quickly and pass it on, the circulation period won't differ—and people will know who has the item in question.

▶ CHANGING REALITY

What makes education real? When people actually change because of new information or new insights about existing information. What makes education authentic? When that change is meaningful, when it transcends the school walls, when it lasts longer than the students' stay in the institution, and when it helps change the "outside" world.

As schools embrace partnerships, educational change increases both in speed and depth. Improvements are more likely to be significant and lasting; fads and fuzzy thinking won't survive the public scrutiny, and good ideas will grow in more fertile ground. Because of partnerships, schools can maintain their integrity in the face of societal change.

The flexible nature of partnerships makes

it easier to accommodate change. There are no rigid barriers to break down. Schools will not crumble in the face of something different. Rather, new ways of doing things, new information, can be assessed critically and incorporated as needed. The core values remain, the "soul" of the school is maintained, but the outside dressing may change. Using the garden metaphor, individual plants may sprout and die, different flowers will blossom with the changing seasons, but the overall garden thrives and gives pleasure to all.

Bibliography

Addesso, P. *Management Would be Easy... If It Weren't for the People.* New York, N.Y.: American Management Association, 1996.

Albritton, R. and T. Shaughnessy. *Developing Leadership Skills.* Englewood, Colo.: Libraries Unlimited, 1990.

American Association of School Librarians. *Collaboration: Lessons Learned.* Chicago, Ill.: American Library Association, 1996.

American Association of School Librarians. *Teaching Through Collaboration.* Chicago: Ill.: American Library Association, 1996.

American Association of School Librarians and the Association for Educational Communication and Technology. *Information Power: Building Partnerships for Learning.* Chicago, Ill.: American Library Association, 1998.

Avino, D. *Librarian Teacher Partnerships.* Cransford, N.J.: Union College, 1994.

Avolio, B. and B. Bass., ed. *Improving Organizational Effectiveness Through Transformational Leadership.* Thousand Oaks, Calif.: Sage Publications, 1994.

Baker, S. and K. Baker. *The Complete Idiot's Guide to Project Management.* New York, N.Y.: Simon & Schuster, 1998.

Bazeli, M. J. *Technology Across the Curriculum: Activities and Ideas.* Englewood, Colo.: Libraries Unlimited, 1997.

Bell, C. *Customers as Partners.* San Francisco, Calif.: Berrett-Koehler Publishers, 1994.

Bodwell, D. *High Performace Team Concept.* Dallas, Tex.: OnRamp Technologies, 1997.

Bramson, R. *Coping with Difficult People.* Garden City, N.Y.: Doubleday, 1981.

Breivik, P. S. and J. A. Senn. *Information Literacy: Educating Children for the 21st Century.* New York, N.Y.: Scholastic, 1994.

Brenton, M. *Lasting Relationships.* New York, N.Y.: Addison & Wesley Publishers, 1981.

Brinkman, R. and R. Kirschner. *Dealing with People You Can't Stand.* New York, N.Y.: McGraw-Hill, 1994.

Bryan, M., J. Cameron and C. Allen. *The Artist's Way at Work.* New York, N.Y.: William Morrow, 1998.

California Assessment Collaborative. *Charting the Course Toward Instructionally Sound Assessment.* San Francisco, Calif.: Far West Laboratory for Research and Development, 1993.

California Media and Library Educators Association. *From Literacy Skills to Information Literacy: A Handbook for the 21st Century.* Castle Rock, Colo.: Hi Willow, 1994.

California School Library Association. *Information Literate in Any Language.* Castle Rock, Colo.: Hi Willow, 1995.

Carkhuff, R. *Sources of Human Productivity.* Amherst, Mass.: Human Resource Development Press, 1983.

Carr, J. *Communicating and Relating.* Menlo Park, Calif.: Benjamin/Cummings Publishing, 1979.

Carr-Ruffino, N. *The Promotable Woman.* 2d ed. Belmont, Calif.: Wadsworth Publishing, 1993.

Cleaver, B. and W. Taylor. *The Instructional Consultant Role of the School Library Media Specialist.* Chicago, Ill.: American Library Association, 1989.

Clifford, D. and R. Warner. *The Partnership Book.* Berkeley, Calif.: Nolo Press, 1996.

Cohen, A. *The Portable MBA in Management.* New York, N.Y.: John Wiley & Sons, 1993.

Conklin, R. *How to Get People to Do Things.*

Chicago, Ill.: Contemporary Books, 1979.

Conroy, B. and B. Schindler Jones. *Improving Communication in the Library.* Phoenix, Ariz.: Oryx Press, 1986.

Conte, C. *The Learning Connection: Schools in the Information Age.* Washington, D.C.: Benton Foundation, 1997.

Costa, A. *Supporting the Spirit of Learning: When Process is Content.* Thousand Oaks, Calif.: Corwin Press, 1997.

Costa, A. and R. Garmston. *Cognitive Coaching: A Foundation for Renaissance Curriculum.* Norwood, Mass.: Christopher Gordon Publishers, 1994.

Covey, S. *Principle-Centered Leadership.* New York, N.Y.: Simon & Schuster, 1991.

Crawley, J. *Constructive Conflict Management.* San Diego, Calif.: Pfeiffer & Company, 1993.

Daniels, A. *Bringing out the Best in People.* New York, N.Y.: McGraw-Hill, 1994.

De Pree, M. *Leadership without Power.* San Francisco, Calif.: Jossey-Bass Publishers, 1997.

Dewar, D. *The Quality Circle Guide to Participation Management.* Englewood Cliffs, N.J.: Prentice-Hall, 1980.

Dinkmeyer, D. and G. McKay. *Parenting Teenagers.* Circle Pines, Minn.: American Guidance Service, 1990.

Doiron, R. and J. Davies. *Partners in Learning.* Englewood, Colo.: Libraries Unlimited, 1998.

Donaldson, G., Jr. and D. Sanderson. *Working Together in Schools.* Thousand Oaks, Calif.: Corwin Press, 1997.

Donham, J. *Enhancing Teaching and Learning.* New York, N.Y.: Neal-Schuman, 1998.

Educational Research Service. "Parent Involvement," *The Informed Educator Series.* 1998.

Eisenhower National Clearinghouse for Mathematics and Science Education. *Ideas that Work: Mathematics Professional Development.* Washington, D.C.: U. S. Dept. of Education, 1998.

Farmer, L. *Cooperative Learning Activities in the Library Media Center.* 2d ed. Englewood, Colo.: Libraries Unlimited, 1999.

Farmer, L. *Informing Young Women: Gender Equity Through Literacy Skills.* Jefferson, N.C.: McFarland, 1996.

Farmer, L. *Leadership Within the School Library and Beyond.* Worthington, Ohio: Linworth Publishing, 1994.

Farmer, L. and W. Fowler. *More Than Information: The Role of the Library Media Center in the Multimedia Classroom.* Worthington, Ohio: Linworth Publishing, 1998.

Feinberg, S. and Sari Feldman. *Serving Families and Children Through Partnerships.* New York, N.Y.: Neal-Schuman, 1996.

Fisher, R. and S. Brown. *Getting Together: Building a Relationship That Gets to Yes.* Boston, Mass.: Houghton-Mifflin, 1988.

Flowers, H. *Public Relations for School Library Media Programs.* New York, N.Y.: Neal-Schuman Publishers, 1998.

Gardner, H. *Multiple Intelligence: The Theory in Practice.* New York, N.Y.: Basic Books, 1993.

Goleman, D. *Working with Emotional Intelligence.* New York, N.Y.: Bantam Doubleday Dell, 1998.

Gossen, D. and J. Anderson. *Rethinking Discipline.* Saskatoon, Canada: Chelsom Consultants, 1999.

Hackman, Mary H. *Library Information Skills and the High School English Program.* 2nd ed. Englewood, Colo.: Libraries Unlimited, 1999.

Hamm, M. and D. Adams. *Cooperative Learning: Critical Thinking and Collaboration Across the Curriculum.* Springfield, Ill.: Charles C. Thomas Publisher, 1996.

Hartzell, G. *Building Influence for the School Librarian.* Worthington, Ohio: Linworth Publishing, 1994.

Haycock, K. *School Library Program in the Curriculum.* Englewood, Colo.: Libraries Unlimited, 1990.

Hellriegel, D., J. Slocum, and R. Woodman. *Organizational Behavior.* 3rd ed. St. Paul, Minn.: West Publishing, 1983.

Hiam, A. *The Vest-Pocket CEO.* Englewood Cliffs, N.J.: Prentice-Hall, 1990.

Higgins, B. J., et al. *Reaching Out: Cooperative Activities for the LMC and Art, P. E., Home Ec., Music, Health, and More.* Englewood, Colo.: Libraries Unlimited, 1990.

Johnson, D. W. and R. J. Johnson. *Learning Together and Alone.* 4th ed. Needham Heights, Mass.: Allyn and Bacon, 1997.

Johnson, S. *Interface Culture: How New Technology Transforms the Way We Create and Communicate.* San Francisco, Calif.: Harper, 1997.

Jones, S and M. Beyerlein, ed. *In Action: Developing High-Performance Work Teams.* Alexandria, Va.: Association for Supervision and Curriculum Development, 1998.

Jweid, R. H. and M. Rizzo. *Library-Classroom Partnership.* Metuchen, N.J.: Scarecrow Press, 1988.

Keirsey, D. and M. Bates. *Please Understand Me: Character and Temperament Types.* Del Mar, Calif.: Prometheus Nemesis, 1984.

Kendall, J. S. and R. J. Marzano. *The Systematic Identification and Articulation of Content Standards and Benchmarks: Update.* Aurora, Colo.: Mid-Continent Regional Educational Laboratory, 1995.

Knowles, E. and M. Smith. *The Reading Connection: Bringing Parents, Teachers, and Librarians Together.* Englewood, Colo.: Libraries Unlimited, 1997.

Krimmelbein, C. *The Choice to Change.* Englewood, Colo.: Libraries Unlimited, 1989.

Kroeger, O. and J. Thuesen. *Type Talk at Work.* New York, N.Y.: Bantam Doubleday Dell, 1992.

Larson, C. E. and F. J. M. LaFasto. *Team Work.* Newbury Park, Calif.: Sage Publications, 1989.

Loertscher, D. V. *Taxonomies of the School Library Media Program.* Englewood, Colo.: Libraries Unlimited, 1988.

Mankin, D., S. Cohen and T. Bikson. *Teams and Technology: Fulfilling the Promise of the New Organization.* Cambridge, Mass.: Harvard Business School Press, 1996.

Marzano, R., D. Pickering and J. McTighe. *Assessing Student Outcomes: Performance Assessment Using Dimensions of Learning.* New York, N.Y.: Elsevier, 1993.

McCain, C. H. *Plugged In and Turned On: Planning, Coordinating, and Managing Computer-Supported Instruction.* Thousand Oaks, Calif.: Corwin Press, 1996.

Melohn, T. *The New Partnership.* Essex Junction, Vt.: Oliver Wight Publications, 1994.

Nierenberg, G. *The Art of Negotiating.* New York, N.Y.: Hawthorn Books, 1968.

Oakes, J. and K. H. Quartz. *Creating New Educational Communities: Schools and Classrooms*

Where All Children Can Be Smart. Chicago, Ill.: National Society for the Study of Education, 1995

Orsburn, J. et al. *Self-Directed Work Teams: The New American Challenge.* Burr Ridge, Ill.: Irwin Professional Publishing, 1990.

Pace, R. and D. Faules. *Organizational Communication.* 3rd ed. Englewood Cliffs, N.J.: Prentice-Hall, 1994.

Perrone, V., ed. *Expanding Student Assessment.* Alexandria, Va.: Association for Supervision and Curriculum Development, 1991.

Phillips, S. and R. Elledge. *Team-Building Source Book.* San Diego, Calif.: Pfeiffer, 1989.

Powell, J. *Why Am I Afraid to Tell You Who I Am?* Niles, Ill.: Argus Communications, 1969.

Rothman, R. *Measuring Up: Standards, Assessment and School Reform.* San Francisco, Calif.: Jossey-Bass Publishers, 1995.

Sange, P. *The Fifth Discipline: The Art and Practice of the Learning Organization.* New York, N.Y.: Doubleday, 1990.

Schaef, A. and D. Fassel. *The Addictive Organization.* San Francisco, Calif.: Harper, 1988.

Schlotes, R., R. Joiner and B. Streibel. *The Team Handbook for Educators.* Madison, Wis.: Joiner Associates, 1994.

Scott, C. *Empowerment: A Practical Guide to Success.* Menlo Park, Calif.: Crisp Publications, 1991.

Senator, R. *Collaborations for Literacy.* Westport, Conn.: Greenwood Publishing, 1998.

Shartrand, A. et al. *New Skills for New Schools: Preparing Teachers in Family Involvement.* Cambridge, Mass.: Harvard Graduate School of Education, 1997.

Shaw, R. *Trust in the Balance.* San Francisco, Calif.: Jossey-Bass Publishers, 1997.

Sheehy, Gail. *New Passages.* New York, N.Y.: Random House, 1995.

Sorrow, Barbara Head. *Multimedia Activities for Students: A Teachers' and Librarians' Handbook.* Jefferson, N.C.: McFarland, 1997.

Spitzer, K. and M. Eisenberg. *Information Literacy: Essential Skills for the Information Age.* Syracuse, N.Y.: Syracuse University, 1999.

Stripling, B. *Libraries For the National Education Goals.* Syracuse, N.Y.: ERIC Clearinghouse on Information Resources, 1992.

Turner, P. *Helping Teachers Teach.* Littleton, Colo.: Libraries Unlimited, 1985.

Umbach, K. W. *Computer Technology in California K-12 Schools: Uses, Best Practices, and Policy Implications.* Sacramento, Calif.: California State Library, 1998.

United States. Department of Education. *A Compact for Learning.* Washington, D.C.: U.S. Dept. of Education, 1997.

United States. Department of Education, Office of Educational Research and Improvement. *Meeting the Technology Challenge: Building New Learning Communities.* Washington, D.C.: U.S. Dept. of Education, 1998.

Urbanik, M. *Curriculum Planning and Teaching Using the Library Media Center.* Metuchen, N.J.: Scarecrow Press, 1989.

Valauskas, E. J. and M. Ertel. *The Internet for Teachers and School Library Media Specialists.* New York, N.Y.: Neal-Schuman, 1996.

Vallacher, R. and A. Nowak. *Dynamical Systems in Social Psychology.* San Diego, Calif.: Academic Press, 1994.

Van Vliet, L. *Media Skills for Middle Schools.* 2d ed. Englewood, Colo.: Libraries Unlimited, 1998.

Vandergrift, K. *Power Teaching: A Primary Role of the School Library Media Specialist.* Chicago, Ill.: American Library Association, 1993.

Weeks, D. *The Eight Essential Steps to Conflict Resolution.* Kirkwood, N.Y.: J. P. Tarcher, 1992.

Weisinger, H. *Emotional Intelligence at Work.* San Francisco, Calif.: Jossey-Bass Publishers, 1997.

Wiggins, G. and Jay McTighe. *Understanding by Design.* Alexandria, Va.: Association for Supervision and Curriculum Development, 1998.

Wilson, B. G., Ed. *Constructivist Learning Environment: Case Studies in Instructional Design.* Phoenix, Arizona University Press, 1996.

Winn, P. G. *Integration of the Secondary School Library Media Center into the Curriculum.* Englewood, Colo.: Libraries Unlimited, 1991.

Young Adult Library Services Association. *Youth Participation in Libraries: A Training Manual.* Chicago, Ill.: American Library Association, 1991.

Zingher, G. *At the Pirate Academy: Adventures with Language in the Library Media Center.* Chicago, Ill.: American Library Association, 1996.

Index

A

AASL (American Association of School Librarians)   17, 30, 78, 81
Access   6, 18, 22, 83-84, 88, 91, 96-98, 100
Accounting   16, 73
Acquisitions   38
Adaptive technology   51-53, 94
Advisors   63
AECT (Association for Educational Communication and Technology)   1
Affiliation   21
Aides   31-32, 41, 45, 96
ALA (American Library Association)   17, 30, 78, 81
AmericaLinksUp   18
American Memory   23
Apple   46-49
Applications   40-41
Archives   5, 23, 65, 95
Art   46, 90, 92
Assessment (see also evaluation)   4-5, 22, 24, 23, 34, 75-78, 82, 85, 90, 93, 95, 103, 105, 106, 109, 113, 117
Assignments (see also lesson plans, research projects)   5, 6, 18, 27, 58, 61, 98, 99
Atmosphere   56, 98, 106
Audience   7, 67, 90, 109
Authority   24

B

Bibliographies   18, 65, 69, 82, 78, 99, 101
Boards (school)   63
Body language   71
Book selection (see also collections)   68
Business   4-5, 49, 115
Budgets   30

C

California   4, 18, 94
Change   116-117
Check It Out!   21-22
Children's Catalog   68
Circulation   27, 42, 104, 116
Coaching   26, 77, 102, 113, 116
Collections   7, 28, 34, 51, 62, 64-66, 68, 89, 91, 98, 102-103, 104, 106, 112, 116
Colleges   45-49
Colorado   18

Commitment   72, 77
Community   45-49, 97
Competencies (see also skills)   6, 87, 103, 105, 116
Computer literacy   19
Conflict   14-15, 73-74, 79
Content   7, 85, 89, 90, 92, 105, 109, 116
Contracts   33
Counselors   28, 94
Credentials   9
Curriculum   18, 20, 47, 63, 64, 77, 86, 89, 96, 102-105
CUSeeMe   23

D

Data   16, 97, 106
Databases   35, 45, 91, 99, 102
Dependability   1
Delivery system   7, 90
Dinkmeyer   15
Displays   65, 95, 105, 114
Districts   21, 42-43
Diversity   94
Dominican College   46-49

E

Equity   93, 100
Engagement (see involvement)
Electric Library   18, 22
Elementary grades   83
English   46
Equipment   29, 46-47, 93
ERIC   18
Ethics   82, 104
Evaluation (see also assessment)   6, 8, 18, 44, 83-84, 88, 102, 110, 112
Events   63, 65-66, 71, 94, 97, 100, 103, 105
Expectations   10, 39, 100

F

First Class   23
Focusing on Learning   105
Food services   28, 65
Foreign language   90, 94, 97-98
Friends of the Library   37
Fund-raising   37-38, 65-66

G

Gifted students 94
Goals 3-, 74
Gossen 15
Governance 20, 36, 51, 63
Great Books 94
Groups 20, 60-61, 78, 85, 92-93, 95, 96, 103, 112-113

H

Harassment 41
High performance teams 16
High school (see also Redwood High School) 84, 107
Homework 99

I

Identity 16
Individuals 16, 20
Information literacy 17-20, 23, 30, 34, 64, 66, 77, 78, 81-87, 97-98, 105
Information Power 1, 18, 22, 30, 78, 81, 106
Instruction 5, 6, 8, 20, 26, 64, 74, 78, 82, 95, 98, 101, 113
Intellectual freedom 103
Internet (see also technology, Web sites) 23, 86-87, 94, 97, 103, 104
Interview 31-32, 39-40, 64, 99, 102
Involvement 16, 36, 76, 95, 113

J

Job description 40
Journalism 47

K

Kansas 18
Knowledge management 16

L

Latinos 4, 90
Leadership in the School Library and Beyond 50
Learning (see also instruction) 4
Learning community (see school community)
Learning style 5, 13
Legalities 30, 104
Lesson plans (see also assignments, research projects) 18, 26, 90, 92
Library Bill of Rights 103
Location (see also space) 7, 90
Lotus: Notes 23
LSTA (Library Services and Technology Act) 51

M

Maintenance staff 28
Mainstreaming (see also diversity, special education) 30
Management 16
Marin County 46, 51
Mathematics 83
Media (see also communication, multimedia, videotaping) 91
Meetings 60, 73, 78
Mentors 20, 30, 79, 108
Middle schools 84
More than Information 14
Multicultural (see diversity, foreign language)
Multimedia 48-49, 82, 92, 96, 102
Music 92

N

National Library Media Month 94
Needs 56-57, 61, 74, 96, 102
Networking 73
New York Times Guide to Children's Reading 68
Newsletter (see also communication) 73
Norms 14, 94
Nurses 28

O

Objectives 7, 15, 40, 89, 90
Obstacles 12, 72-74, 76, 111
Organizations 20, 88, 115
Orientation 42-43
Outcomes 5, 17, 23, 85, 92, 109

P

Pacing 71, 113
Parents 19, 36, 67-69, 94, 97, 100, 104
Pathways 61-62, 98
Peers (see also coaching, tutoring) 50
Perceptions 9-10
Personality 11-13, 72, 76, 79
Personalization 4
Photography 47, 92
Placement 31
Planning process 7, 14, 21-22, 26-27, 75, 77, 88, 100, 105, 111-113, 116
Policies 40-41, 78, 103
Portfolios 48, 76, 78
Powell 13
Primary grades 83
Primary sources 24
Problem-solving 15, 29, 74

Products   65-66, 88, 95, 113
Public libraries   50, 81
Purpose   13-14

R

Read-Aloud Handbook   68
Reader's Guide   86
Reading   16, 17, 30, 56, 61-69, 78
Reform   17, 30, 116
Research projects (see also assignments, lesson plans)   5, 18, 20, 23, 64, 82, 88, 90, 95, 101, 105
Resignation   41
Resources (see collections)
Responsibility   16, 23, 40
Risk-taking   72
Roles   79, 115-116
Rubrics   5, 16, 18-19, 77

S

Safety   41
Scavenger hunt   59
Scheduling (see also time)   7, 27, 78, 90, 93, 96, 100
School community   4, 10, 25, 61, 64-66, 73, 87, 102, 105
School culture   10
School-to-work   46-49
Search engines (see Internet)
Secretaries   28
Self-knowledge (see also personality)   11-12
Services   58-60, 64, 91, 106-107
Simulations   85, 113
Site-based management   30
Skills   18, 31-32, 34, 39, 47, 61, 85, 87, 96, 97, 100, 116
Social interaction   13, 20, 20, 75
Society   4
Socio-economics   24
Space (see also location)   71
Speakers   92, 97
Special education (see also diversity, mainstreaming)   51-53, 94, 98
Staff development (see also training, workshops)   18, 19, 48, 71, 73, 106-107
Standards   17-19, 22, 105, 106
Student teachers   45, 87
Students   5-6, 14, 18, 23-24, 31-35, 47, 50, 61, 81-82, 85-87, 90, 94, 95, 98, 104

Supervision   6, 30, 44, 115
Support   10, 11, 16, 17, 30, 80, 94, 105
Support staff   28, 50, 72, 75
Supreme Court   85
Surveys (see also assessment, evaluation)   37, 56, 58, 106-107
Systems   73, 76, 115-116

T

Tasks   9, 15-16, 20, 23, 60-61, 71, 74, 82, 96-97
Teachers   5-8, 14, 18-19, 25-27, 30, 45, 47-48, 60-61, 86-87, 106
Team-teaching   64
Technology (see also Internet, Web sites)   17-19, 23, 28, 31-32, 45, 52, 61, 65, 71, 74-75, 78, 83-84, 87, 88, 91, 94-96, 105, 106, 111-113
Technology specialists   6, 14, 28, 100, 106
Telecommunications   23
Tests   5, 16
Time   16, 72, 76, 90, 112
Time frame   7, 101
Training (see also staff development, workshops)   42-43, 47-48, 52, 96, 108, 111-113
Training Student Library Staff   29, 35
Trelease   68
Trust   11, 14-15
Tutoring   34-35, 94
Type Talk at Work   12

U

Ultimate Reader   92
University of California, Berkeley   24
University of Virginia   24

V

Videotaping   34, 48, 61, 83, 93, 96, 97, 102, 114
Volunteers   39-44

W

WASC (Western Association of Schools and Colleges)   17, 22, 47, 105
Web sites   18-19, 24, 27, 34, 45, 56, 65, 71, 92, 94, 105, 114
Wednesday Surprise   67
Why Am I Afraid to Tell You Who I Am?   13
Work experience   31
Workshops (see also staff development, training)   13, 18, 67-69, 108-113
Workshops for Teachers   70

www.ingramcontent.com/pod-product-compliance
Lightning Source LLC
Chambersburg PA
CBHW082224010526
44113CB00037B/2499